Better Homes and Gardens®

Old-Fashioned Christmas Crafts

Better Homes and Gardens® Books
Des Moines, Iowa

Better Homes and Gardens® Books
An Imprint of Meredith® Books

OLD-FASHIONED CHRISTMAS CRAFTS
Senior Editor: Carol Spier
Editor: Ron Harris
Technical Editor: Ellen Liberles
Associate Editor: Ruth Weadock
Copy Editor: Sydne Matus
Associate Art Director: Lynda Haupert
Contributing Designer: Linda Vermie
Creative Editorial Coordinator: Karin Strom
Production Manager: Bill Rose
Photographs: George Ross
Illustrations: Roberta Frauwirth, Laura Hartman Maestro

Vice President and Editorial Director: Elizabeth P. Rice
Executive Editor: Maryanne Bannon
Art Director: Ernest Shelton
Managing Editor: Christopher Cavanaugh

President, Book Group: Joseph J. Ward
Vice President, Retail Marketing: Jamie L. Martin
Vice President, Direct Marketing: Timothy Jarrell

Meredith Corporation
Chairman of the Executive Committee: E. T. Meredith III
Chairman of the Board and Chief Executive Officer: Jack D. Rehm
President and Chief Operating Officer: William T. Kerr

All of us at Meredith® Books are dedicated to offering
you, our customer, the best books we can create. We
are particularly concerned that all of our instructions
for making projects are clear and accurate. Please
address your correspondence to
Customer Service
Meredith Press
150 East 52nd Street
New York, NY 10022.

Contents

Introduction

Much of what makes an old-fashioned Christmas so appealing lies in togetherness with family and friends, warm sentiments, timeless stories, and favorite traditions. Providing the backdrop for such a happy holiday are the vivid, aromatic, and myriad decorations and gifts that can ornament the house from top to bottom: a traditional pyramid tree featuring unique Christmas memorabilia, glittering gilded ornaments shaped like stars, or perhaps a fantastically decorated gingerbread house spilling over with sweets and icing, delighting young and old alike.

◆

Old-Fashioned Christmas Crafts lets you re-create these and dozens of other charming, traditional Christmas projects while using modern, convenient methods. There are gifts and accessories here for every room in the house and everyone on your list, from a classic cross-stitched pillow for the living room to personalized patchwork stockings that children will love—all inspired by styles ranging from Victorian to country, Renaissance to folk art, Mother Nature to Father Christmas.

◆

The Christmas season lends itself perfectly to the nostalgic and the romantic, to sharing cherished memories while creating new ones. It's a time to begin new traditions and celebrate old ones, so your children will know the joy of an old-fashioned Christmas too. We hope you enjoy creating an old-fashioned Christmas in your home.

Father Christmas

'Twas the night before Christmas,
when all through the house
Not a creature was stirring,
not even a mouse;
The stockings were hung
by the chimney with care,
In hopes that St. Nicholas
soon would be there.

A spry embodiment of generosity, Santa
Claus is a heart-warming figure to
young and old. The jovial toymaker's character
has evolved from that of the fourth-
century bishop Nicholas, who became
the patron saint of children. Known for his
benevolence, he distributed gifts to
them and performed other charitable acts wher-
ever he traveled. Over the years
his image developed into that of a sometimes
stern Father Christmas and, eventually,
into the jolly fellow we know today.

Pinecone Father Christmas

This Santa is a direct descendent of the German Father Christmas figures made between 1870 and 1920, which were considered the height of holiday fashion in many American households. Like the traditional figures, he bears valuable gifts—a tree, a bag of fruit, and an abundance of goodwill.

Size
Father Christmas is 13" tall.

Materials
- Assorted large pinecones
- Wooden base, 6" diameter
- Acrylic paint: red and gold
- Foam paintbrush, 1" wide
- Small amount of wool fleece: white
- Small amount of fake fur: natural brown
- Netting, 2" × 4"
- Assorted trims, ¼" wide
- Small amount of polyester stuffing
- Porcelain Santa head and hands (with long neck and partial forearms)
- Felt doll's hat to fit head
- Doll boots, 2" tall: black
- Miniature Christmas toy sack, presents, sled, and toys
- Miniature Christmas tree, 4" tall
- Dollhouse Christmas lights for tree
- 20 wooden balls, ½" diameter
- Decorative twigs, 3½" long
- Pruning shears
- Florist's wire
- Wire cutters
- Hot-glue gun and glue sticks

Directions
Cover the work surface with newspaper and plastic wrap and keep a roll of paper towels handy. Allow paints to dry thoroughly between steps.

Base: Paint the base red, then paint a thin coat of gold. Using a paper towel, wipe the paint off as desired, leaving streaks of gold. Paint the rim gold.

Figure: Follow Figure 1 for the placement of the pinecones. Using the pruning shears, cut 2 narrow pinecones to 4-inch lengths for the legs. Glue the boots onto the smaller ends. Wire the top ends together, wrapping the wire inconspicuously between the scales on the pinecones. Glue the boots centered on the base. Cut off the top of a wide pinecone, leaving a 3-inch length for the body. Glue the head onto the pointed end. Glue the cut end of the body on top of the pinecone legs.

Pick 2 curved and narrow (about 1½ inches in diameter) 4-inch-long pinecones for the arms. If necessary, narrow the arm pinecones by picking away the scales along one side (which will be against the body), leaving only the core. Set aside the scales. Trim off the pointed ends of the arm pinecones and glue the hands there. Glue loose scales around the top edge of the hands to cover the joining. Glue the arms in place on the body. Split 2 pinecones, each about 3 inches long, in half lengthwise for the vest. Glue 2 pieces to the front and 2 pieces to the back of the body to round it out.

Trims: Arrange and glue the wool fleece in place on the Santa face for the side hair, mustache, and beard. Cover the felt hat with fake fur and glue in place. Glue the hat in place on the head. Fill the toy sack with polyester stuffing. Glue trim around the top of the sack. Following the photograph, glue the sack to Santa's back at the right shoulder. Arrange and glue the miniature sled, toys, and presents coming out of the sack and onto the shoulder. Glue the twigs to Santa's left hand. Glue the tree to Santa's right hand. Glue the tiny Christmas lights scattered on the tree.

In a small jar, dilute red paint with water. Place the wooden balls in the diluted red paint and let them sit until they turn the desired color for apples. Drain them and allow them to dry. Fold the 2- by 4-inch piece of netting in half crosswise and glue the short edges and the bottom edge together to make a net bag. Turn it right side out, then fill it with the wooden apples. Wire the top closed and glue a piece of trim around the top of the net bag with a 2-inch end to extend over Santa's left shoulder. Glue the bag and shoulder strap in place.

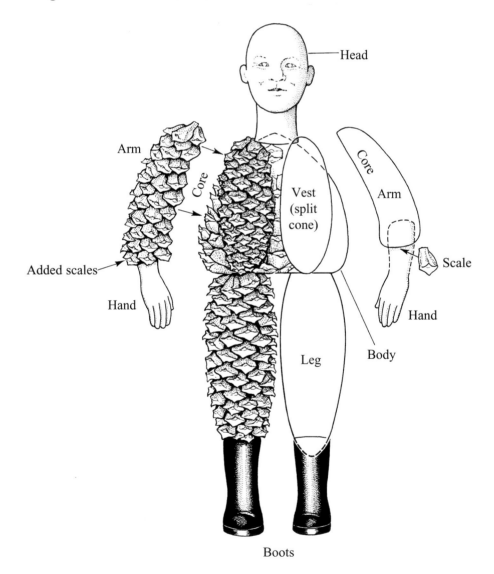

Figure 1

Hooked Santa Picture

*The technique of rug hooking
creates a textural country Santa. Traditionally,
strips of old woolen clothing were used, but
this picture can be made from new wool
fabrics such as flannel and gabardine.
The muted colors give it an antique appearance.*

Size
Hooked picture is 16" square.

Materials
✦ 22" square of 8-oz. or 10-oz. burlap
✦ Rug hook
✦ Rug-hooking frame or large wooden hoop
✦ Closely woven wool fabric: white, cream, light gray, light pink, yellow, gold, gold tweed, red, green, very dark green, and black for the motifs; closely related blues and grays for the background
✦ 2 yd. of rug binding, $1\frac{1}{2}$" wide
✦ Carpet thread
✦ 16" square of particle board, $\frac{1}{4}$" thick
✦ Fine permanent marker: black
✦ Tracing and transfer papers
✦ Staple gun and staples
✦ Picture-hanging hardware
✦ Masking tape

Directions
Preparation: Before you begin your project, please read "Enlarging Patterns" and "Transferring Patterns," pages 185 and 186. Cover the edges of the burlap with masking tape to prevent raveling. Enlarge the pattern. This project is hooked with a traditional rug hook from the right side, so you do not need to reverse the design. Transfer the pattern onto the burlap. Outline the pattern with the permanent marker. Mark a 16-inch square for the outside edges. Cut the wool into $\frac{1}{4}$-inch-wide strips. Wool that will be used for finely detailed areas, such as the stars, moon, tree, face, fur, trim, and hat, should be cut into $\frac{1}{8}$-inch-wide strips. The strips shouldn't be longer than 12 inches. To determine the amount of wool needed for each area, allow enough fabric to cover 4 to 5 times the area to be hooked.

Hooking: Place the burlap taut in the frame or wooden hoop. Hold the hook in one hand on the top side and the wool in between your thumb and forefinger in the other hand on the underside of the fabric. Insert the hook from the top side through the burlap to the wrong side, catch the end of the fabric strip on the hook (Figure 1), and pull up the fabric end to the top side (Figure 2). Skip 2 threads of burlap. Insert the hook from the top side through the burlap to the wrong side and pull up a $\frac{1}{4}$-inch fabric loop to the top side (Figure 3). Skip 2 threads and pull up a second loop. Continue to work as established, keeping all loops $\frac{1}{4}$ inch high and even, until the fabric strip is finished. Pull up the end to the top side, then begin a new strip.

Work the motifs first. Follow the photograph for color placement, or work as desired. First outline the section to be worked; then fill in the section. When each motif is finished, work 1 row of the background color around it to maintain the shape. After all the motifs have been worked, work 1 row of a contrasting color (we used red) around the marked outside edges of the 16-inch square. Fill in the background area, varying the colors of the strips for a mottled, antique effect. Trim the excess ends even with the loops.

Edging: Remove the burlap from the frame. Trim the burlap to $1\frac{1}{2}$ inches from the edges of the hooked design. Hem the raw edges of the burlap to prevent raveling. Slipstitch the rug binding to the burlap around the edge of the hooked design. Steam-press with a very damp cloth on the right side. Allow to dry thoroughly.

Mounting: Stretch your work over the particle board and fold the excess burlap and binding to the wrong side of the board. Using the staple gun, secure the piece to the board. Attach the picture-hanging hardware.

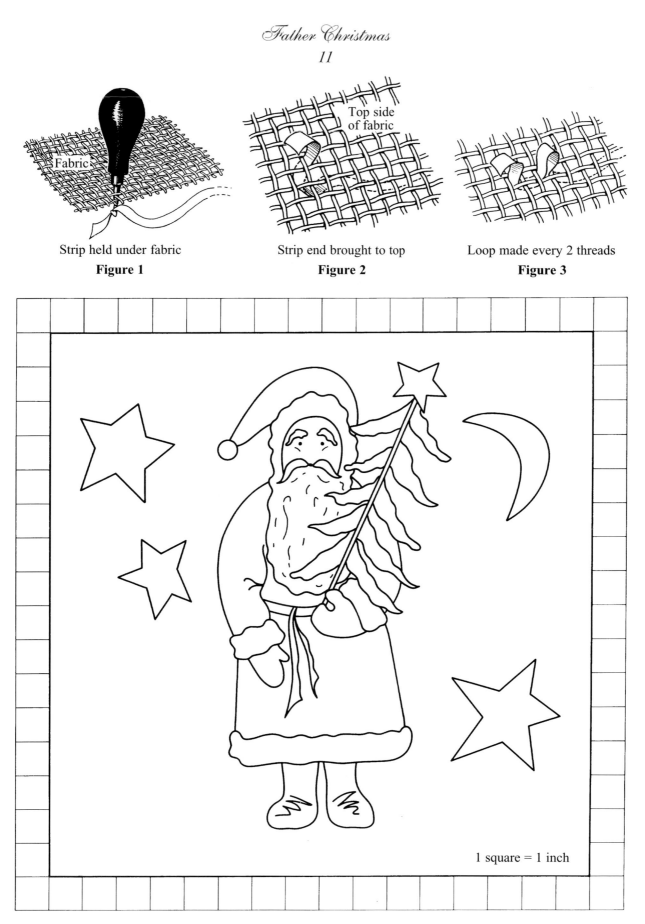

Fabric

Strip held under fabric

Figure 1

Top side
of fabric

Strip end brought to top

Figure 2

Loop made every 2 threads

Figure 3

1 square = 1 inch

Hooked Santa Picture Pattern

Father Christmas Cornucopias

Cornucopias make wonderful holiday gifts or party favors that guests can take home and hang on their tree. These examples are Victorian in style and origin and were used as holders for candies and other small treats.

Size
Cornucopias are 5" to 6".

Materials
✦ Gold foil doilies, 10" to 12" diameter, or gold foil
✦ Assorted Christmas stickers or motifs cut from gift wrapping paper
✦ Sequins
✦ Assorted Christmas trims and twisted cords
✦ Small bookmark tassels: assorted colors
✦ Small stapler and staples
✦ Compass
✦ Crafts glue and glue sticks

Directions
Use gold foil doilies, or mark 10- to 12-inch-diameter circles on the foil with a compass and cut them out. For all cornucopias, fold the circles into quarters and cut at the folds. Four cornucopias are made from each circle. Place the cut edges together with a ½-inch overlap to make a cone shape. Do not crease. Staple together at the top edge and glue the remaining seam in place to secure. Cut 2 pieces of desired trim to fit around the inside and outside of the top edge. Glue in place.

Cut 9-inch strips of desired trim for the handles. Glue the ends to the top edge on each side of the cornucopia. Glue on sequins to cover the cut edges of the handles. Glue stickers or gift wrap motifs to the front of the cornucopia. Glue a tassel at the point of the cornucopia. Fill with candy, nuts, or small favors as desired.

Theorem-Painted Santa Stocking

Popular in the United States in the early nineteenth century, theorem painting uses layers of stencils to create rich, multicolored designs. Cotton velveteen is the best material for this technique because the nap absorbs the paint so well. The paint is dabbed on in small amounts using a piece of fabric as a brush, creating a subtle, shaded effect. This handsome Santa could also be adapted for a decorative pillow.

Sizes
Stocking is 15" tall.

Materials

✦ 1⅛ yd. of velveteen fabric (not treated with Scotchgard®): cream
✦ ¾ yd. of lining fabric: cream
✦ 1⅛ yd. of twisted cord, ⅜" in diameter, with flange: white
✦ 2¼ yd. of twisted cord, ³⁄₁₆" in diameter, with flange: green
✦ 6" length of gold-edged ribbon, ⅝" wide: green
✦ Contrasting and matching threads
✦ 1 small tube each of oil paint: alizarin crimson (A), cobalt blue (B), oxide of chromium green (C), yellow ocher (D), ivory black (E), cerulean blue (F), burnt umber (G), cobalt violet (H), and cadmium yellow light (I)
✦ Fine paintbrush
✦ Turpentine
✦ Palette or paper plate
✦ Poster board
✦ Stencil paper
✦ Crafts knife
✦ Dressmaker's pencil
✦ Tracing and transfer papers
✦ Spray adhesive
✦ Rubber cement
✦ Masking tape

Directions

Note: Before you begin your project, please read "Enlarging Patterns," page 185, and "Transferring Patterns" and "Making Stencils," page 186. For all seams place fabric pieces with right sides together and make ½-inch seams (unless otherwise directed). Keep a roll of paper towels handy. Spray the poster board with adhesive to use as a work surface. Paints do not need to dry thoroughly between painting steps.

Theorem Painting: Cut off a 12-inch-wide strip across velveteen and reserve to make "brushes." Enlarge the stocking pattern. Using the dressmaker's pencil, transfer the pattern to the right side of one-half of the remaining velveteen for the front. With contrasting thread, mark the crosses where indicated for the stencil register marks. Press the marked velveteen right side up onto the prepared poster board.

Trace the 5 separate stencil layers onto stencil paper. Include the stencil register marks. Number the stencils 1 through 5, indicating the order in which the stencils will be worked. Cut out the stencils. Cover the back of the stencil paper with rubber cement. Allow to dry. Tape the first stencil in place on the velveteen with masking tape, matching stencil register marks.

Cut nine 6-inch squares from the reserved velveteen. You will wrap one around your finger, nap side out, to paint each color. Cover any exposed areas of velveteen to protect them from paint smears, adjusting the covering when you change stencils. If you have not tried theorem painting before, you may want to practice first on scrap velveteen fabric before starting your stocking.

Squeeze the paint onto the palette with the colors at least 1 inch apart from one another so they don't mix. The theorem painting technique uses little paint, so begin with too little paint on your fingertip velveteen brush rather than too much. Blot any excess paint from the fabric brush onto a paper towel. Clean your fingers with turpentine often so you don't mix colors.

Working in a circular motion, press the velveteen brush lightly against the stocking fabric to paint the design area. Work from the edges of the stencil toward the center, leaving the center as lightly colored as desired. Keep the velveteen free from lint by using masking tape to remove lint particles.

When you finish working one layer of stencil, remove it. Tape the next stencil layer in place, matching the stencil register marks, and proceed to paint as before. Continue until all 5 layers of stencils are worked (for the fourth stencil, see "Facial Details," below). If gaps remain between the stenciled areas, reposition the stencils and add paint.

Facial Details: With a pencil, lightly mark the facial details shown on Stencil Pattern 4. Remove the stencil. Following the photograph, use the fine paintbrush to paint the nose, hair, and beard lines with G, the eyes with F, and the cheeks and the mouth with A. Follow the photograph to add additional details, outlining Santa's hands, sleeve cuffs, and left forearm with the fine paintbrush, or a fine-line permanent marker, if you find it easier to use. Also outline other edges (such as gifts in Santa's pack) as desired to give greater definition to the design. Allow to dry for 48 hours before assembling the stocking.

1 square = 1 inch

Stencil register 1

Stencil register 2

Theorem-Painted Santa Stocking Pattern

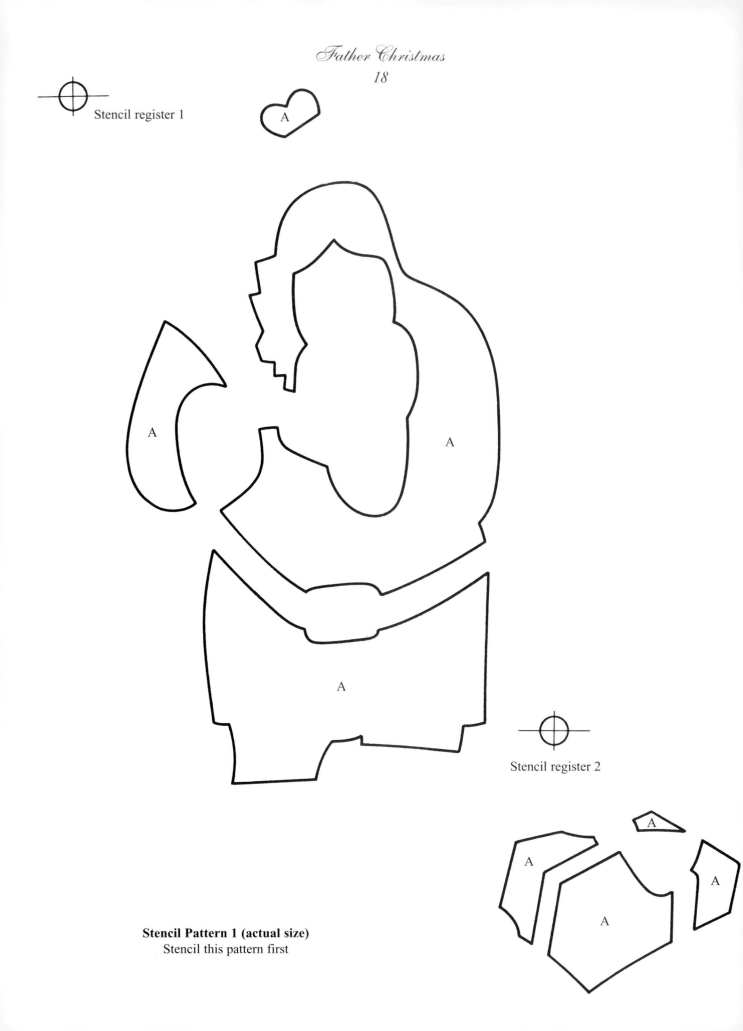

Father Christmas
18

Stencil register 1

A

A

A

A

A

A

A

A

Stencil register 2

Stencil Pattern 1 (actual size)
Stencil this pattern first

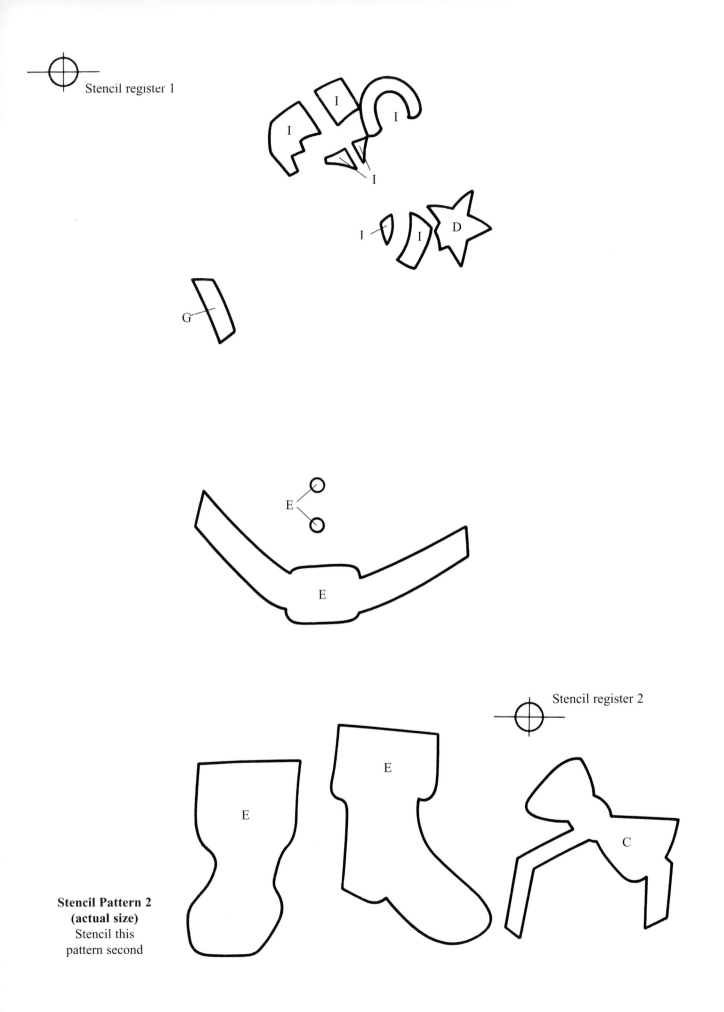

Stencil register 1

I

I

I

I

I

I

D

G

E

E

Stencil register 2

E

E

C

**Stencil Pattern 2
(actual size)**
Stencil this
pattern second

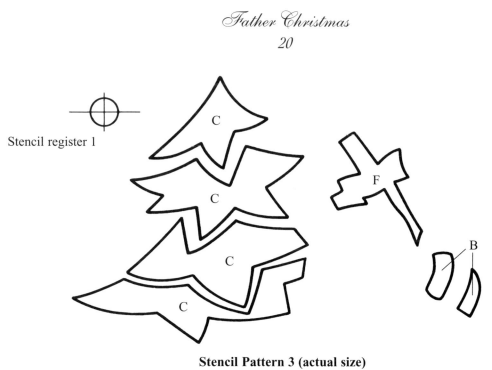

Stencil register 1

Stencil Pattern 3 (actual size)
Stencil this pattern third

Stocking: Fold and pin the velveteen fabric in half. Cut out the stocking through both layers of fabric. Cut out a 4½- by 18-inch piece for the cuff. Fold the lining fabric in half and transfer the stocking pattern to it. Cut out the stocking lining through both layers; cut out the cuff lining, making it same size as cuff.

Assembly: If needed, trim the green cord flange to ½ inch. Aligning the raw edges and with green cord toward the center, pin the cord around the edges on the right side of the painted front piece, easing the cord to fit (Figure 1). Using a zipper or cording foot and a ⅜-inch seam allowance, sew around the edges. In the

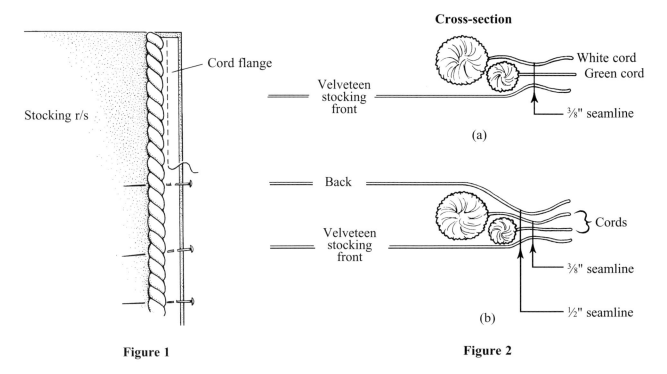

Figure 1

Figure 2

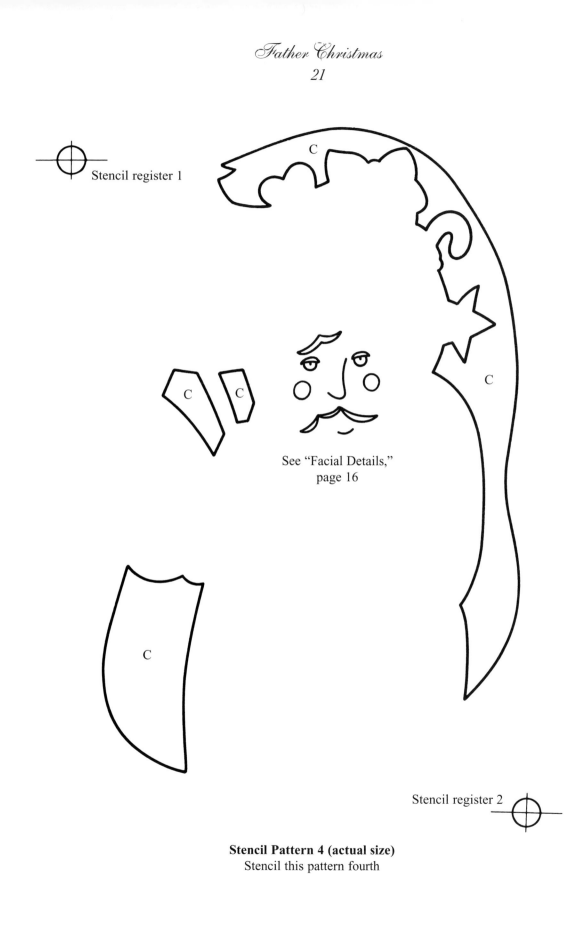

Stencil register 1

C

C

C

C

C

C

See "Facial Details,"
page 16

Stencil register 2

Stencil Pattern 4 (actual size)
Stencil this pattern fourth

Stencil register 1

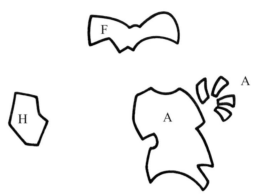

Stencil Pattern 5 (actual size)
Stencil this pattern fifth

same manner, position the white twisted cord over the green cord, with the white cord lying inside the green (Figure 2a). Sewing over the previous seam line, stitch in place. Clip the curves. With right sides together, both cords sandwiched between the layers, and stitching a ½-inch seam or as close as possible to the green cord (Figure 2b), sew the back to the front of the stocking, leaving the top edge open. Sew the stocking lining pieces together, leaving the top edge open. Trim the seams and clip the curves. Turn the stocking right side out. With the wrong sides together, slip the lining inside the stocking. At the top of the stocking, turn in the raw edges ½ inch and slipstitch the lining to the stocking all around the top opening.

Cuff: Aligning the raw edges and with the green cord toward the center, pin the cord on the right side of each long edge of the vel-

veteen cuff. Using a ⅜-inch seam allowance, sew the cord in place.

Pin cuff to cuff lining along one long edge. Sew them together, stitching as close to the cord as possible. Open out the pieced unit. Fold the cuff unit in half crosswise and sew across the ends to form a tube. Turn the velveteen section of the cuff to the right side so the seamed edge with the cord forms the bottom edge. At the other corded edge (top of the cuff), turn in the seam allowances and slipstitch the cuff and the cuff lining together. Slip the cuff over the stocking and slipstitch it in place around the top opening. Fold the 6-inch length of ribbon in half for a hanging loop. Tack the ends inside the top of the stocking at the back seam.

Fleece Father Christmas

*Ornaments fashioned from scraps of cotton
batting were popular in the nineteenth century.
Less precious than breakable glass ornaments,
fabric ornaments were hung on the lower branches
of the Christmas tree so that curious children
could play with them safely. The ornaments shown
here are reminiscent of a popular German
design of the day.*

Size
Ornament is 9" tall.

Materials
- 10" × 12" piece of fleece for each ornament: red or white
- Scrap of felt: white or red (use contrasting color to fleece)
- Scrap of cotton batting
- 8" × 10" piece of cardboard for each ornament
- Wrapping paper or card with Santa face
- Miniature teddy bear
- Decorative twigs and evergreens
- Metallic pipe cleaner: gold
- Tracing paper
- Spray adhesive
- Crafts glue

Directions
Enlarge the Santa pattern and transfer the body outline onto the cardboard (see "Enlarging Patterns" and "Transferring Patterns," pages 185 and 186). The broken lines on the pattern indicate the position of the pieces added later. Cut out 1 Santa shape for each ornament. Spray the front of the cardboard shape with adhesive and cover it with fleece. Repeat on the back of the cardboard. Trim the fleece to the shape of the cardboard.

Cut out the Santa face from the wrapping paper or card. Using spray adhesive, glue it in place. Cut a small piece of cotton batting for the beard and glue it in place. From the fleece, cut two 1- by 9-inch pieces, one 1- by 5-inch piece, and one ½- by 6-inch piece. Following the photograph and the broken lines on the pattern, fold the 5-inch piece in half lengthwise; with the fold facing forward, wrap it around the top of the face for the hood. Glue in place. Glue the 6-inch piece down the cen-ter of the front. For the coat collar, wrap one long piece around the entire shape, beginning and ending at the front and covering the ends of the hood. Glue in place. For the arms, wrap the second long piece below the collar and around the entire shape. Glue the ends in place.

Position a small teddy bear, wreath, or twigs in the arms and glue in place. From the contrasting-color felt, cut 2 mittens and glue them in place for the hands. Fold a 6-inch piece of pipe cleaner in half. Glue the ends to the top back of the ornament for a hanging loop.

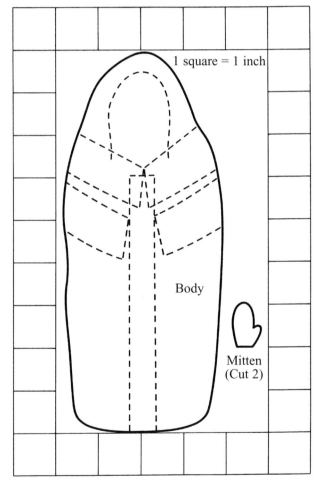

1 square = 1 inch

Body

Mitten (Cut 2)

Fleece Father Christmas Ornament Patterns

Victorian Crazy-Quilt Stocking

*The crazy quilt is a free-form and
decorative way to use and show off fancy
fabric scraps such as velvets, satins, and brocades,
which make a luxurious backdrop for favorite
embroidery stitches. This oversized stocking
features lavish fabrics, specialty stitches, and
punch-needle embroidery.*

Size
Stocking is 23" tall.

Materials
- 28" × 30" piece of muslin
- 31" × 30" piece of velveteen fabric for backing
- 1 yd. of lining fabric
- 28" × 30" piece of lightweight batting
- Scraps of velveteen, moiré, satin, silk, patterned fine corduroy, cotton, polished cotton, or desired fabrics
- Three 12" squares of tightly woven cotton muslin
- 1 yd. of crocheted lace edging
- Contrasting and matching threads
- 6-strand embroidery floss: assorted colors for embroidery and Santas
- Kreinik Metallic Thread, #8 Braid: iridescent white, black, and assorted shades of green
- Punch needle, 1-strand size
- 6" to 8" screw-type embroidery hoop
- Glass beads and beading needle
- Assorted decorative mother-of-pearl buttons
- Fray Check
- Cardboard
- Tracing and transfer papers
- Fabric glue

Directions
Note: Before you begin your project, please read "Enlarging Patterns" and "Transferring Patterns," pages 185 and 186. For all stitched seams, place fabric pieces right sides together and make ¼-inch seams (unless otherwise indicated). Enlarge the stocking pattern and transfer the outline for 2 stockings onto the lining fabric, reversing it once. Cut out the lin-ing pieces. Transfer the stocking pattern onto the backing (with the toe pointing right on the right side of the fabric); cut the piece out. Transfer the stocking pattern onto the muslin, with the stocking toe pointing left. Do not cut out the muslin stocking. Trace the crazy-quilt patterns and transfer them onto the cardboard for templates; cut them out. Do not reverse the templates. Draw the shapes onto the right side of the fabric scraps, adding ⅛-inch overlap all around. Cut out the pieces, numbering them on the wrong side.

Patchwork: Arrange the fabric scraps on the muslin, overlapping the edges. Trim the overlaps so the punch-needle designs will fit onto the appropriate patches. Heavier fabrics should overlap lighter-weight ones. Dab the edges with Fray Check to prevent fraying. Pin and baste the patches in place. Topstitch ¼ inch inside the marked edge of the stocking.

Embroidery: Following the photograph, use floss to secure the seams of the patches with the desired embroidery stitches (see "Embroidery Stitches," pages 188 to 190). Writing freehand, personalize the stocking with the desired name and date, adding flow-ers to patches as indicated. Embroider the designs. Sew on the beads and buttons, fol-lowing photograph for placement. Leave enough space for the punch-needle designs, which will be worked separately and glued on later. Remove basting threads.

Stocking: Sew the stocking lining pieces together, leaving the top edge open. Clip the curves. Place the pieced stocking front right side up over the batting. With contrasting thread, baste the layers together along the

1 square = 1 inch

1

2

3

4

5

6

7

Date

8

9

10

Buttons

11

12

Name

13

14
Buttons

15

16

17

18

19

20

21

Victorian Crazy-Quilt Stocking Pattern

stitching line around the edge. This will be used as a guide when attaching the backing. Cut out the stocking shape, leaving a ¼-inch seam allowance beyond the stitching line. Sew the backing fabric to the stocking front along the stitching line, leaving the top edge open. Clip the curves and turn right side out. With wrong sides together, place the stocking lining inside the outer stocking.

Measure around the top opening. Baste across the top edge of the lace edging and pull the thread to gather the lace to fit the top opening. Slipstitch the short edges of the lace together. Aligning the raw edges and centering the seam at the center back, pin and sew the lace around the opening of the stocking.

For the binding, cut a 2½-inch-wide strip of backing fabric 14 inches longer than the opening measurement. Fold the strip in half lengthwise. Stitch across one short edge, then 9 inches along the long edge (Figure 1). Leave the opening measurement unstitched. Sew the last 5 inches and the opposite short edge

(Figure 1). Turn right side out. Begin at the back seam of the stocking and bind the top opening of the stocking with the unstitched section of the binding, leaving the stitched ends extending at the back seam. For a hanging loop, fold the 9-inch stitched end of the binding into a loop (Figure 2) and tack it in place. Leave the 5-inch stitched end free.

Punch-Needle Embroidery: Transfer the Santa motifs onto the wrong side of the muslin (note that the designs are reversed because you will be working from the wrong side). With the wrong side facing you, stretch the fabric taut in the embroidery hoop. Following the punch-needle manufacturer's instructions, work the design from the back of the fabric. Follow the photograph for floss colors or work in desired colors. Highlight areas with metallic threads as desired. Trim the fabric to the edge of the design. Glue the motifs in place on the front of the stocking with fabric glue.

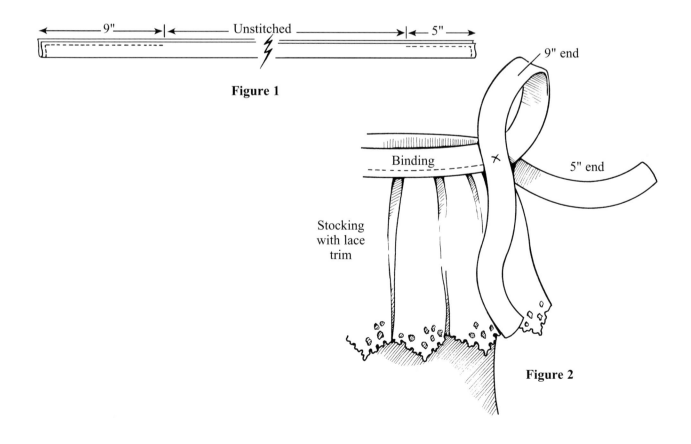

Figure 1

Figure 2

Punch-Needle Embroidery Patterns
(actual size)

Velvet Santa Star Ornaments

Victorian in style and sentiment, these whimsical ornaments are soft, cuddly, and unbreakable. They will brighten any tree and appeal to all ages.

Size

Ornaments are 6" tall.

Materials

+ Two 8" squares of velvet for each ornament
+ Small amount of tea-dyed muslin (see "Dyeing with Tea," page 187)
+ Polyester stuffing
+ Small amount of paper-backed fusible web
+ 6" length of cord for each ornament, $\frac{1}{8}$" diameter: gold
+ Matching thread
+ Wool doll hair: white
+ Glitter pen: gold
+ Fine marker: black
+ Cosmetic blush and cotton swab
+ Tracing and transfer papers
+ Crafts glue

Directions

Preparation: Trace all the patterns. Transfer the face pattern onto the paper backing of the fusible web (see "Transferring Patterns," page 186). Following the manufacturer's instructions, fuse the web to the wrong side of the tea-dyed muslin. Cut out the face shape. Cut 2 star shapes and 2 hats from the velvet. Fuse the muslin face in place on the right side of one star; do not place the iron on the velvet. With the black marker, draw 2 dots on the face for the eyes. With the cotton swab, apply a small amount of cosmetic blush to the cheeks.

Assembly: With *wrong* sides together, work a narrow zigzag stitch around the edges of the star, leaving the top of the face open for stuffing. Stuff lightly, using a chopstick or other stuffing tool to fill the points of the star. With the glitter pen, draw over the zigzag stitching lines on the velvet. Color in the points of the star. Glue the doll hair around the open top and below the eyes for the hair and beard, then allow to dry.

With right sides together and making $\frac{1}{4}$-inch seams, sew the hat pieces together, leaving the lower edge open. Turn right side out and stuff lightly. Turn $\frac{1}{4}$ inch of the lower edge to the wrong side and tack the hat in place on the head. With the glitter pen, paint the tip of the hat gold. Paint a single line of gold along the lower edge and decorate with gold dots as desired. Allow to dry. Fold the 6-inch length of cord in half. Tack in place at the back of the head for a hanging loop.

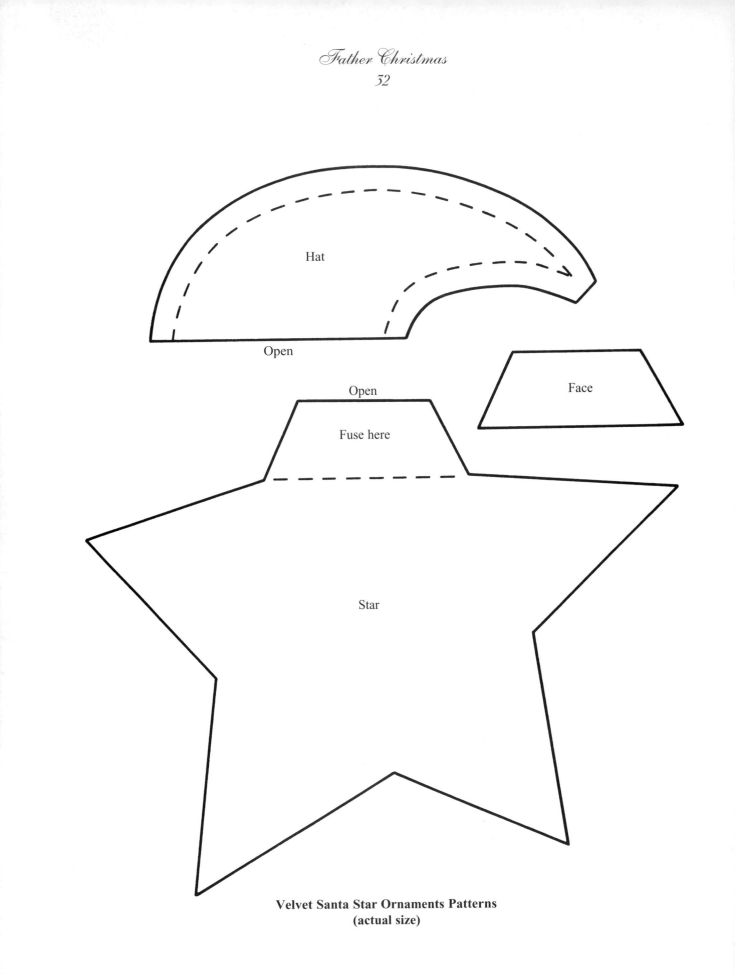

Hat

Open

Open

Fuse here

Face

Star

Velvet Santa Star Ornaments Patterns
(actual size)

A Celestial Christmas

Hark! the herald angels sing,
"Glory to the newborn King."

Angels—whether majestic
messengers from above, reminiscent
of those lavishly depicted in
Renaissance art, or the simplified,
more down-to-earth angels seen in
American folk art—are often a
favorite of Christmas connoisseurs.
In these projects they appear in
all shapes, sizes, and styles, bringing
both glad tidings and a sense
of the spiritual side of an often hectic
holiday season.

Golden Angels Table Runner

Stylized flying angel and star motifs suggest European embroidered textile designs. Stenciling is a quick way to create a rich holiday look, and the gold metallic paint gives this Golden Angels Table Runner an elegance that blends with the most sophisticated decor.

Size
Runner is 15" × 44".

Materials
- ✦ ½ yd. of linen fabric, 45" wide: off-white
- ✦ ½ yd. of fine cotton fabric for lining, 45" wide: off-white
- ✦ Matching thread
- ✦ Fabric paint: gold
- ✦ Stencil brushes, ½" diameter
- ✦ Stencil paper
- ✦ Dressmaker's pencil
- ✦ Tracing and transfer papers
- ✦ Crafts knife
- ✦ Rubber cement
- ✦ Masking tape, 1" wide

Directions
Note: Cover the work surface with newspaper and plastic wrap and keep a roll of paper towels handy. Allow the paint to dry thoroughly between steps.

Cutting: Cut one 16- by 45-inch rectangle from the linen and one from the cotton. With right sides together and using a ½-inch seam allowance, sew the linen and cotton pieces together, leaving an opening for turning along one short edge. Trim the seams to ¼ inch. Turn right side out and press. Slipstitch the opening closed. Tape the piece, linen side up, securely onto your work surface. Using masking tape, mark off 1 inch around the edges. Leaving a ¼-inch band uncovered, place another row of masking tape around the edges, parallel to and inside the first row (Figure 1).

Stenciling: Enlarge the star and angel designs and trace them onto the stencil paper (see "Enlarging Patterns" and "Making Stencils," pages 185 and 186). Cut out the stencils. Cover the back of the stencil paper with rubber cement. Allow to dry. Before you begin your project, practice on scrap paper or fabric, working as follows: Blot any excess paint from the brush onto a paper towel. Stamp the brush in an up-and-down motion to achieve a crisp, clean edge. Working from the edges of the stencil toward the center, leave the center blank, lightly colored, or solidly colored, as desired. To prevent smears, allow paints to dry and be sure the stencil edges are not wet when you move the stencil. When you are comfortable with your results, you are ready to begin your project.

Paint the ¼-inch band left uncovered around the edges with gold for the border. Allow the paint to dry and then remove the masking tape. Mark the horizontal and vertical centers of the runner with the dressmaker's pencil. Following the photograph, position the stencil along the marked center lines and stencil the pattern. Lining up the stencil where marked, stencil the angel pattern 3 times from the center toward one short edge. Rotate the stencil. Starting again at the center line, line up the stencil to complete the center stars on the other side of the runner and stencil the center star pattern. Then, working from the center to the opposite short edge, repeat the angel design 3 times, so that the angels face in the opposite direction. Allow paint to dry. Following the manufacturer's instructions, heat-set the paint.

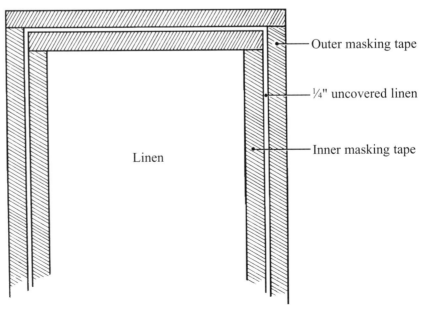

Figure 1

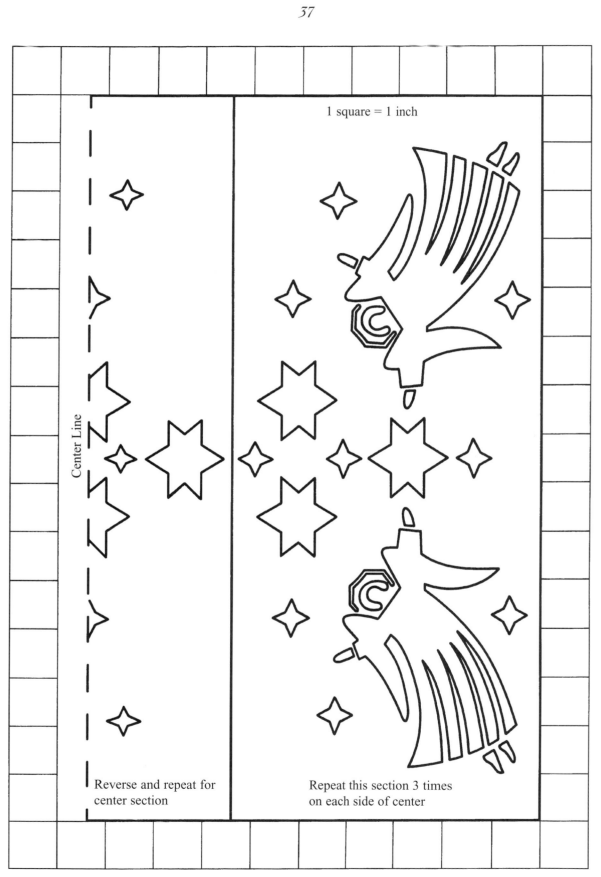

1 square = 1 inch

Center Line

Reverse and repeat for center section

Repeat this section 3 times on each side of center

Golden Angels Table Runner Stencil Pattern

Flying Brass Angels

A popular motif in American folk art,
angels are magnificent even
in simple outline. These trumpeting
Flying Brass Angels are easy to cut from
fine-gauge brass sheets and make a delightful
holiday mobile, or they can be given
as gifts or hung on the tree as ornaments.

Size

Angel is $3\frac{3}{4}$" × $8\frac{1}{2}$".

Materials

✦ .005" × 4" × 10" sheet of brass for each angel, from hardware or art supply store

✦ Brass wire

✦ 28" length of wire-edged reversible ribbon for each angel, $\frac{1}{8}$" wide: red and green with gold edges

✦ Tin snips with sharp blades

✦ Hammer and nail

✦ Tracing paper

✦ Crafts knife

✦ Spray adhesive

Directions

Enlarge the angel pattern and trace it (see "Enlarging Patterns," page 185). Cut 1 tracing paper pattern for each angel. Spray the back of each pattern with adhesive and press it smoothly onto a brass sheet. Using tin snips, cut out the angel shape. Working on a board or self-healing mat to avoid damaging your table, use the crafts knife to cut out the area between the arm and the horn, changing blades as needed. Use the hammer and nail to punch the hole as marked for the hanging ribbon. Thread the 28-inch length of ribbon through the hole and tie the ends into a bow. Trim and shape the ends as desired. To attach to a chandelier, wrap brass wire around the center of the bow and around the chandelier.

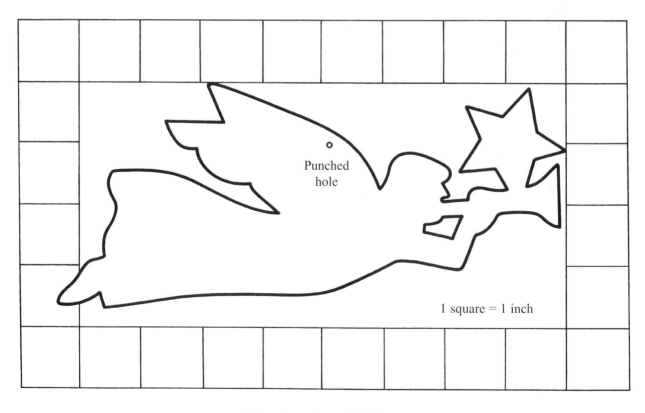

Punched hole

1 square = 1 inch

Flying Brass Angels Pattern

Twinkling Star Tree Skirt

A galaxy of shining and falling stars is stenciled onto shimmering taffeta, giving this brilliant tree skirt a lustrous glow. The skirt is lined in a contrasting color and tied around the base of the tree with matching star-covered ribbon.

Size
Tree skirt is 54" in diameter.

Materials
✦ 1¾ yd. of taffeta fabric, 60" wide: burgundy
✦ 1¾ yd. of iridescent taffeta fabric, 60" wide: teal
✦ ½ yd. of ribbon, 1½" wide: burgundy with gold stars
✦ Matching thread
✦ Fabric paint: gold metallic
✦ Stencil brushes, ½" diameter
✦ Stencil paper
✦ Dressmaker's pencil
✦ Tracing and transfer papers
✦ Crafts knife
✦ Rubber cement
✦ Yardstick with hanging hole at one end
✦ Pushpin

Directions
Cover the work surface with newspaper and plastic wrap and keep a roll of paper towels handy. For ease in working, tape the fabric to the work surface. Allow paints to dry thoroughly between steps.

Skirt: Spread out the burgundy fabric flat on the floor with wrong side up. Use the yardstick as a compass by inserting the pushpin through the hole and into the center of the fabric. Attach the dressmaker's pencil with a rubber band 27½ inches from the pinpoint. Swing the

yardstick and pencil around in an arc to draw the outer circle (Figure 1). Draw a second circle 3 inches from the pinpoint for the inner circle. Cut out the 55-inch-diameter circle for the top of the skirt. From the teal fabric, cut out a 57-inch square. With the right sides of the burgundy circle and the teal square together and using a ½-inch seam allowance, sew around the outer circle. Stitch along the marked line of the inner circle.

Using the yardstick, mark a line from the outer circle to the inner circle for the back slit. Stitch ½ inch in along each side of the marked line, leaving a 6-inch opening for turning on one side. Cut along the marked line and inside the inner circle, leaving a ½-inch seam allowance. Trim the excess fabric around the

outer circle; notch the outer curves and clip the inner curves. Turn the skirt right side out and press. Turn in the raw edges and slipstitch the opening closed. Cut the ribbon in half. To make ties, tack one end of each piece to each corner at the inner circle edge of the back slit. Trim the ends as desired.

Stenciling: Enlarge and transfer the star pattern to the stencil paper (see "Enlarging Patterns" and "Making Stencils," pages 185 and 186). Cut out the stencil. Cover the back of the stencil paper with rubber cement. Allow to dry. Before you begin your project, practice on scrap paper or fabric as follows: Blot any excess paint from the brush onto a paper towel. Stamp the brush in an up-and-down motion to achieve a crisp, clean edge. Working from the edges of the stencil toward the center, leave the center blank, lightly colored, or solidly colored, as desired. To prevent smears, allow paints to dry and be sure the stencil edges are not wet when you move the stencil. When you are comfortable with your results, you are ready to begin your project.

Position the stencil on the front piece. Stencil stars around as desired, moving the stencil as needed. Cover any exposed fabric not being stenciled with newspaper to protect it while stenciling. Following the manufacturer's instructions, heat-set the paint.

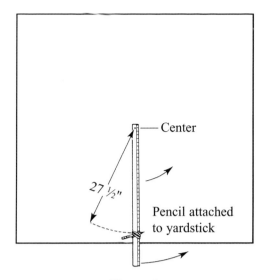

Center

27 ½"

Pencil attached
to yardstick

Figure 1

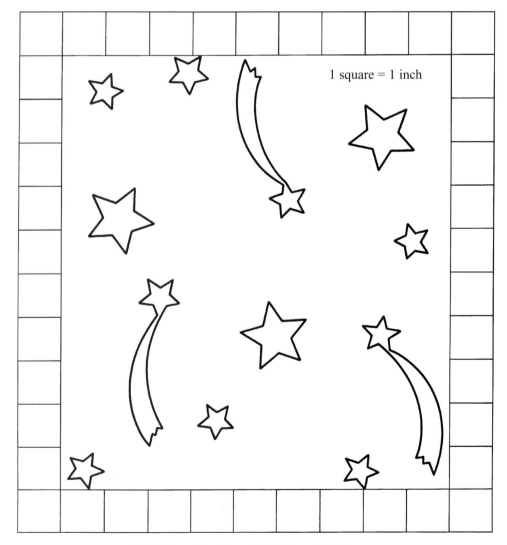

1 square = 1 inch

Twinkling Star Tree Skirt Stencil Pattern

Stencil Star Stocking

Eight-pointed stars and golden jewels and swirls, all on a rich blue moiré background, light up the Stencil Star Stocking. Stars are stenciled on and fanciful details are added as desired.

Size
Stocking is 16" tall.

Materials
+ ½ yd. of moiré fabric: blue
+ ½ yd. of lining fabric: blue
+ ½ yd. of ribbon, ⅜" wide: gold
+ 8" length of braid, ⅛" diameter: gold
+ Matching thread
+ Soft fabric paint: gold metallic
+ Glitter pen: gold metallic
+ Rhinestones, 7 mm and 12 mm: gold
+ Stencil brushes, ½" diameter
+ Stencil paper
+ Dressmaker's pencil
+ Tracing and transfer papers
+ Paper for pattern
+ Crafts knife
+ Rubber cement
+ Crafts glue

Directions
Note: Cover the work surface with newspaper and plastic wrap and keep a roll of paper towels handy. Allow paints to dry thoroughly between steps. Before you begin work on your project, please read "Enlarging Patterns," page 185, and "Transferring Patterns" and "Making Stencils," page 186. For all seams, place fabric pieces together and make ½-inch seams (unless otherwise indicated).

Cutting: Enlarge the stocking pattern. From the moiré fabric, cut out two stockings, reversing one. Repeat with the lining fabric.

Stenciling: Trace the star and the diamond border patterns onto the stencil paper. Cut out the stencil. Cover the back of the stencil paper with rubber cement. Allow to dry. Before you begin your project, practice on scrap paper or fabric as follows: Blot any excess paint from the brush onto a paper towel. Stamp the brush in an up-and-down motion to achieve a crisp, clean edge. Working from the edges of the stencil toward the center, leave the center blank, lightly colored, or solidly colored, as desired. To prevent smears allow paints to dry and be sure the stencil edges are not wet when you move the stencil. When you are comfortable with your results, you are ready to begin your project.

Position and stencil the border onto the front stocking piece. Position and stencil 4 stars. Following the manufacturer's instructions, heat-set the paint. Cut the ribbon in half and glue it in place at the top and bottom edges of the diamond border area.

Assembly: Sew around the edges of the stocking, leaving the top edge open. Repeat for the stocking lining. Trim the seams and clip the curves. Turn the stocking right side out and press. Slip the lining inside the stocking, wrong sides together. Turn in ½ inch around the top edges of the stocking and lining; slip-stitch the edges together. Fold an 8-inch length of braid in half, knot it 2½ inches below the fold, and tack the knot and the ends inside the back seam of the stocking for a hanging loop.

To decorate the front of the stocking, position the rhinestones, following the photograph, and glue them in place. Using the dressmaker's pencil, draw swirls and other desired designs onto the front of the stocking. Pressing firmly and evenly, redraw the designs with the glitter pen.

1 square = 1 inch

Ribbon

Ribbon

Stencil Star Stocking Pattern

Diamond Border Stencil

Star Stencil

Stencil Star Stocking Stencil Patterns
(actual size)

Molded-Paper Angels

These pretty and unpretentious ornaments,
based on traditional angel designs, are
made with simple clay cookie molds. Tied
with ribbon or raffia, they make perfect party
favors, and children will enjoy helping to
make the paper by hand.

Sizes

Ornaments shown are 5" to 6".

Materials

- Angel and angel-with-trumpet terra-cotta cookie molds
- Artist's paper with high rag content, such as watercolor or charcoal
- Tissue paper to add color if desired
- ½ yd. of ribbon for each angel, ¼" wide: gold
- Piece of fine screening or cheesecloth to cover bowl
- Flat paintbrush, ½" wide
- Beeswax
- Kitchen blender
- Bowl
- Double boiler (for melting beeswax)
- Kitchen sponge
- Crafts glue
- Spray sealer

Directions

Paper Making: Tear the paper into small pieces (about the size of a fingernail). Add tissue paper for color as desired (use only one color for each batch). Soak the paper in water overnight or in boiling water for 1 hour to break down the fibers. Working with a small handful at a time, add the paper to 2 cups of water in the blender. Blend for 15 to 30 seconds until the paper becomes pulp. Do not overblend. Some small bits of paper that have not broken down will add character and texture. Fit the screening or cheesecloth over the bowl and pour the paper mixture onto it to drain the water. Press the pulp with your hand to remove as much water as possible.

Ornaments: Melt the beeswax in the double boiler. *Do not melt it in a pan directly over a flame because beeswax is flammable.* Using a paintbrush, coat the inside of each mold with a thick layer of beeswax.

Place the pulp in the mold, pressing it flat into the recesses and covering the mold completely. Using a slightly moistened sponge, press over the entire area to help remove excess water and to push the paper into the details of the mold. Wringing out the sponge as necessary, continue to press the inside of the mold until the paper is as dry as possible. (The paper in the mold should be about the same thickness as lightweight cardboard.) Place the mold in an oven set on the lowest temperature and leave it for ½ to 1 hour, until the paper is completely dry. The edges will begin to rise from the mold. (The paper can also air-dry but will take at least overnight to do so.) Remove the paper from the mold. When the paper is completely dry, spray with the sealer.

Finishing: Cut the ribbon into 9-inch lengths and tie half of the pieces into bows. Trim the ends as desired and glue them to the tops of the ornaments. Fold the remaining pieces of the ribbon in half and glue the ends to the back at the top of each ornament for a hanging loop.

Glory to God Pillow

With flowing robe and a resounding message of joy, this classic cross-stitched angel graces a beautifully decorative pillow. Its delicate design and elegant tones add a touch of splendor to any decor.

Size
Pillow is about 14" × 17".

Materials
✦ 20" square piece of Lugana® 25-count fabric: antique white
✦ ¼ yd. of print fabric: blue metallic
✦ ½ yd. of solid fabric: blue
✦ 1 skein each of 6-strand embroidery floss (see key for colors)
✦ 1 skein of fine, metallic thread: gold
✦ 1 skein each of fine, braided opalescent thread: mauve, yellow, and blue
✦ ½ yd. of iron-on interfacing
✦ Contrasting and matching threads
✦ Polyester stuffing
✦ 2 yd. of caterpillar trim, ½" wide: light gold
✦ 4 tassels, 4": white
✦ Embroidery hoop and needle

Directions
Cross-stitching: See "How to Cross-stitch" and "Embroidery Stitches," pages 187 and 188. With contrasting basting thread, mark the horizontal and vertical centers of the fabric. Center the cross-stitch design on the fabric, matching the fabric center with the arrows on the chart. Following the chart and key, embroider the design. Work cross-stitches with 3 strands of floss over 2 threads; work backstitches with 1 or 2 strands of floss, as indicated in parentheses in key. After the embroidery is finished, carefully remove the basting threads and gently hand-wash the fabric in cold water. Dry it flat and press it on the wrong side using a press cloth.

Assembly: Following the manufacturer's instructions, fuse the interfacing to the back of the cross-stitched piece. Trim the stitched piece to 11 by 13½ inches with the design centered and about ¾ inch extending beyond the design border on all sides. From the print fabric, cut two 3- by 19½-inch pieces for the side borders and two 3- by 17-inch pieces for the top and bottom borders.

With right sides together, matching centers of edges, position and pin the side borders along the opposite long edges of the stitched piece, with the excess of the borders extending equally beyond each edge of the stitched piece. Using a ½-inch seam allowance, sew along the long edges, beginning and ending at the adjoining seam line (½ inch in from the top and bottom edges). Open out the borders; press. In the same manner, position and pin the top and bottom borders to the stitched piece; sew between the corners.

Miter the corners as follows: Fold the pillow diagonally at the corner and place the adjoining border strips right sides together, matching edges. Stitch across the border strips at a 45-degree diagonal from the corner seam line outward to the outer border edge (Figure 1). Trim any excess fabric, leaving a ½-inch seam allowance. Pin and neatly hand-sew the

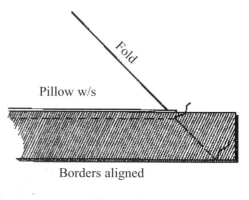

Pillow w/s

Fold

Borders aligned

Figure 1

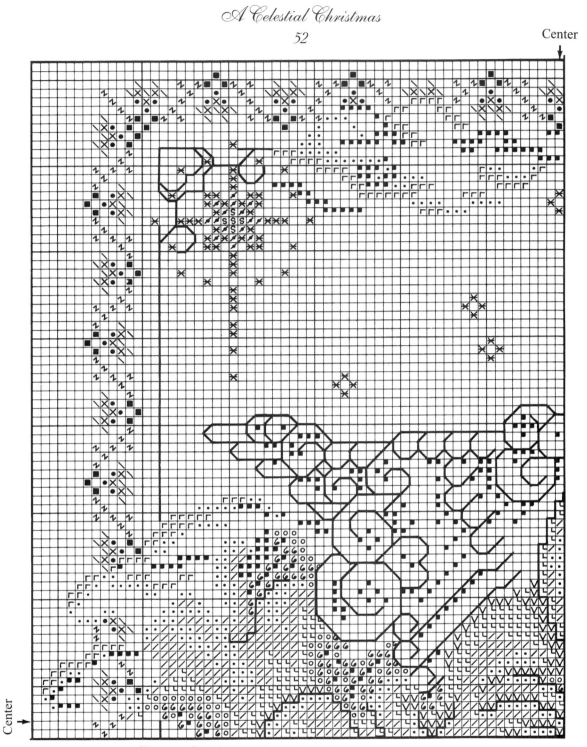

Center

Glory to God Pillow Cross-stitch Chart (top left section)

KEY

Anchor		DMC	Color
2	⌐	Blanc	White
176	6	793	Cornflower Blue Medium
131	V	798	Delft Dark
136	L	799	Delft Medium
928	/	3761	Sky Blue Very Light
158	•	747	Sky Blue Ultra Very Light
878	■	501	Blue Green Dark
262	◢	3363	Pine Green Medium
214	⩘	368	Pistachio Green Light

Anchor		DMC	Color
859	+	523	Fern Green Light
42	●	309	Rose Deep
38	⊠	335	Rose
73	•	963	Dusty Rose Ultra Very Light
882	T	758	Terra Cotta Very Light
868	I	3779	Terra Cotta Ultra Very Light
1046	╲	435	Brown Very Light
362	—	437	Tan Light

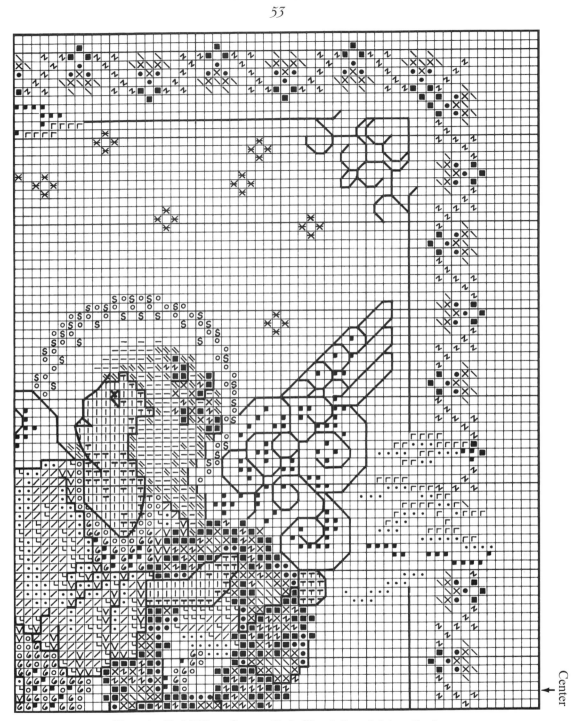

Glory to God Pillow Cross-stitch Chart (top right section)

Anchor		DMC	Color
295	O	726	Topaz Light (3) + Kreinik Blending Filament 002BF Gold (1)
300	✔	745	Yellow Light Pale

KREINIK		**#8 Fine Braid**	
	S	094	Star Blue
	■	093	Star Mauve
	✕	091	Star Yellow

Anchor		DMC	Color
			BACKSTITCH
131	⌐	798	Delft Dark, gown (1), letters (2)
136	⌐	799	Delft Medium, inner wings (2)
175	⌐	794	Cornflower Blue Light, outer wings (2)
42	⌐	309	Rose Deep, border, wreath (1)
360	⌐	898	Coffee Brown Very Dark, face (1)

Glory to God Pillow Cross-stitch Chart (lower left section)

Center

Anchor	DMC	KEY Color
2	Blanc	White
176	793	Cornflower Blue Medium
131	798	Delft Dark
136	799	Delft Medium
928	3761	Sky Blue Very Light
158	747	Sky Blue Ultra Very Light
878	501	Blue Green Dark
262	3363	Pine Green Medium
214	368	Pistachio Green Light

Anchor	DMC	Color
859	523	Fern Green Light
42	309	Rose Deep
38	335	Rose
73	963	Dusty Rose Ultra Very Light
882	758	Terra Cotta Very Light
868	3779	Terra Cotta Ultra Very Light
1046	435	Brown Very Light
362	437	Tan Light

Overlap from adjacent section

Center

Glory to God Pillow Cross-stitch Chart (lower right section)

Anchor		DMC	Color
295	⃝	726	Topaz Light (3) + Kreinik Blending Filament 002BF Gold (1)
300	✦	745	Yellow Light Pale

	KREINIK	#8 Fine Braid
S	094	Star Blue
■	093	Star Mauve
✕	091	Star Yellow

Anchor		DMC	Color
			BACKSTITCH
131	└	798	Delft Dark, gown (1), letters (2)
136	└	799	Delft Medium, inner wings (2)
175	└	794	Cornflower Blue Light, outer wings (2)
42	└	309	Rose Deep, border, wreath (1)
360	└	898	Coffee Brown Very Dark, face (1)

caterpillar trim in place on the front over the border seam line, as shown in the photograph.

Finishing: From the solid blue fabric, cut the back to the same dimensions as the front. With right sides of the front and back together and using a ½-inch seam allowance, sew around the edge of the pillow, leaving a 6-inch opening for turning. Turn right side out and stuff. Slipstitch the opening closed. Sew a tassel to each corner.

Heavenly Screen Angels

Inspired by Renaissance papier-mâché angels, these Heavenly Screen Angels make clever use of commonly available materials. Pliable screening is easily fashioned into gilded robes. Personalize each angel with added trim and accessories to complete a musical trio or a solo angel.

Sizes
Angels are 12" to 13" tall.

Materials
- 3 plastic foam cones, 11" tall
- 3 plastic foam balls, 2" diameter
- 1½ yd. of fiberglass screening, 36" wide
- ½ yd. of fine wire screening
- Wire, 16 gauge
- 2 yd. of cord, ¼" diameter: gold
- 3 yd. of gauze ribbon, 3" wide: gold
- 24" length of gathered lace, 1" wide
- 2 miniature trumpets: gold
- Metallic pipe cleaners: gold
- Acrylic gel medium
- Spray paint: gold
- Acrylic paint: light brown and light pink
- Paintbrushes, medium and #2 pointed
- Foam paintbrush, 1" wide
- Very fine marker: black
- China marker or crayon
- Three 12"-square-based corrugated cardboard boxes for work surface
- 1½" × 3½" piece of stiff paper
- Straight pins
- 3 large rubber bands
- Tin snips
- Hot-glue gun and glue sticks
- Newspaper

Directions

Body: Cover the cardboard boxes with plastic wrap to use as a work surface. Cut 1 inch off the base of one cone so that the cone measures 10 inches tall. With tin snips, cut two 12½- by 36-inch pieces of fiberglass screening and one 11½- by 36-inch piece. Using one large cone and one large piece of screening, wrap the long edge around the cone, overlapping the short edges by 1 inch. Gather, pleat, and drape the screening, using pins to hold it in place at the top of the cone. Use 20 to 25 pins and push them into the cone at a downward angle so they don't come out the opposite side of the cone. Repeat this process with the second large piece of screening and second large cone and with the smaller piece of screening and smaller cone. Measure 3 inches down from the top of each cone and wrap a rubber band around tightly for the waist. Set each angel on a cardboard box and continue working downward to arrange the folds and pleats of the screening as desired, pinning them into the box and the cone to secure them. When the screening is arranged, use the foam brush to paint 2 coats of acrylic gel medium, using more in the deeper folds and allowing it to dry between coats. Remove the pins and take the angel body from the box.

Enlarge the sleeve pattern and, using the china marker, transfer it 6 times onto the fiberglass screening (see "Enlarging Patterns" and "Transferring Patterns," pages 185 and 186). Cut out the sleeves. Fold each one into a cone shape, overlapping the long edges ¼ inch; glue in place, leaving the top 1 inch open. Cut

three 15-inch lengths of wire. On each angel, push one end of wire through the angel and out the opposite side for the arms. Fold the ends of the wire back to form the hands. Slip the sleeves onto the arms and pin them to the body. Fold back the sleeve cuffs and drape the sleeves as desired. Cut the gathered lace into three 8-inch pieces. Gather and arrange a piece around the top of each cone. Glue in place for the collar. Spray-paint each angel body gold, painting the collar as well as under the collar. Allow to dry. Cut the gauze ribbon into 3 pieces. Tie a piece around each waist over the rubber band and tie a bow at the back.

Enlarge the wing pattern and transfer 3 wing designs onto the wire screening, mark-

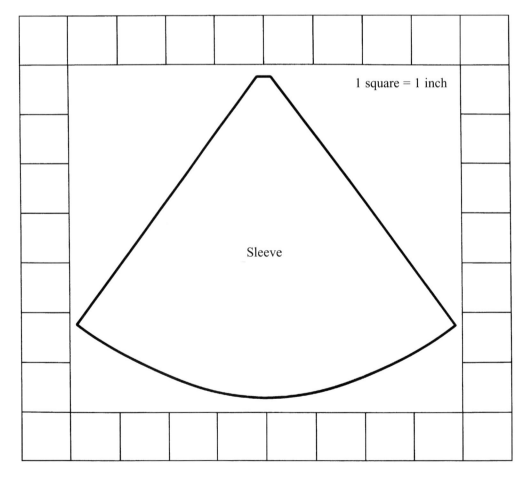

1 square = 1 inch

Sleeve

Heavenly Screen Angels Pattern

ing the screen with the china marker or crayon. Reverse the pattern and draw 3 opposite wing designs. Cut them out. Spray-paint the wings gold. Allow to dry. Glue pipe cleaners all around the shaped edge on the front of the wings. Fold back the wings where marked and pin them to the center of the back.

Head: Using the medium paintbrush, paint the plastic foam balls with 2 or 3 coats of light pink. Allow them to dry. Cut three 2-inch lengths of wire. Push one end into each angel body and the other into an angel head. Glue the head in place. Starting at the back base of the head, pin one end of the cord into the ball to secure it and wrap the cord around the head

in a spiral until the crown is covered. Cut away any excess cord and glue the ends. Repeat this on each angel. Using the pointed paintbrush, paint the cheeks light brown. Using the fine marker, draw details on the face.

Hands: Cut the newspaper into strips, each 1 by ¼ inch. Dip the strips into the gel medium and wrap them around the hands until covered. Allow them to dry, then paint them light pink. Spray-paint the 1½- by 3½-inch piece of stiff paper gold. Allow to dry, then fold the paper in half crosswise for a music book. Position the trumpets and the music book on the angels as desired and glue in place.

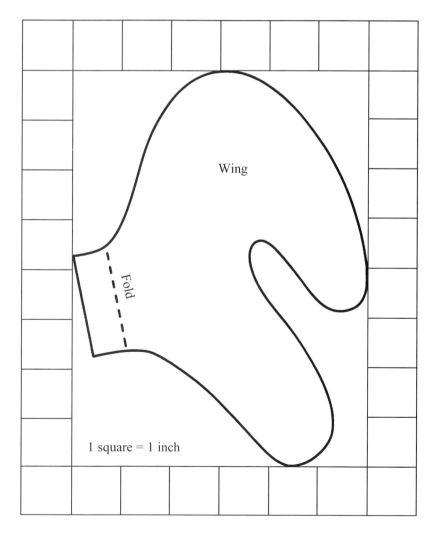

Wing

Fold

1 square = 1 inch

Heavenly Screen Angels Pattern

Littlest Angel Photo Ornament

Every Littlest Angel Ornament becomes a show-case for cherubic young ones. Each child or grand-child will feel like a star. (And you may well start a favorite family tradition!)

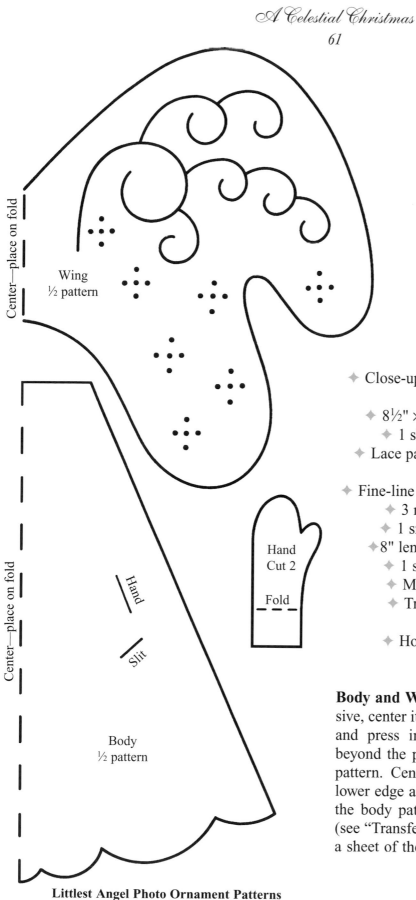

Wing
½ pattern

Center—place on fold

Center—place on fold

Hand

Slit

Body
½ pattern

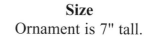

Hand
Cut 2

Fold

Littlest Angel Photo Ornament Patterns
(actual size)

Size
Ornament is 7" tall.

Materials
✦ Close-up photo of child, with face about 2" long
✦ 8½" × 11" pad of parchment paper
✦ 1 sheet of Bristol board, 1 ply
✦ Lace paper doily with medallions, 10" diameter: white
✦ Fine-line fabric-paint pens: gold and pearl
✦ 3 ribbon rosebuds: off-white
✦ 1 small ribbon bow: off-white
✦ 8" length of ribbon, ¼" wide: gold
✦ 1 strand of tiny pearls: white
✦ Metallic pipe cleaners: gold
✦ Tracing and transfer papers
✦ Spray adhesive
✦ Hot-glue gun and glue sticks

Directions
Body and Wings: Spray the doily with adhesive, center it over a sheet of parchment paper, and press in place. The doily will extend beyond the parchment paper. Trace the body pattern. Centering the medallions along the lower edge as shown in the photograph, mark the body pattern on the doily and cut it out (see "Transferring Patterns," page 186). Spray a sheet of the parchment paper with adhesive

and attach it to the Bristol board. Trace the wing pattern, transfer it to the parchment and Bristol board, and cut it out. Transfer the wing designs onto the wing and redraw them with gold and pearl paint as desired. Allow to dry. Glue the string of pearls all around the front edge of the wings. Center the top part of the body over the lower edge of the wings and glue it in place.

Collar and Hands: From the Bristol board, cut out a 2½- by 9½-inch rectangle. Fold it accordion style every ½ inch. Along one side, staple each fold ¼ inch from one edge to hold the folds in place. Fan out opposite edge for collar. Centering the stapled end of the collar on the wings and fanning out the bottom over upper body, glue stapled side of collar in place. Trace hand pattern, transfer it twice to parchment paper, and cut out 2 hands. Fold them where marked and glue in place with folded flap toward the center of the body.

Final Trims: Decorate the body by gluing pearls along the sides, a rosebud in the center of each medallion, and a rosebud between the medallions near the lower edge of the body. Paint the body with the fabric-paint pens as desired. Allow to dry. Cut slits in the body for book inserts where marked. Cut a 1¼- by 3-inch piece of Bristol board and fold it in half crosswise for a book. Decorate the front with paint as desired. Allow to dry. Slip lower corners of the book into slits on body. Cut out the child's face from the photograph and glue it over the top edge of the collar. From the pipe cleaner, make and secure a small circle to fit around the photo head, leaving one long end for the halo stem. Fold the halo stem down and glue it to the back of the wings, with the halo over the child's head. Glue the bow at the center of the neck. Knot ends of gold ribbon together for a hanging loop. Glue knot to back of wings.

Angelic Wrappings

Before commercial wrapping paper was widely available, creating clever wrappings was an essential element of gift giving. Today friends and family will appreciate the artistic quality of these hand-decorated Angelic Wrappings. Simple star and angel stencils make this an easy last-minute project—and one that the littlest angels in the household can help with.

Sizes
Gift wraps, bags, cards, and tags are assorted sizes and as desired.

Materials
✦ 22" × 32" sheets of assorted decorative art and rice papers
✦ Dry-brush stencil paint: medium blue, yellow, gray, and white
✦ Acrylic paint: gold metallic and pearl white metallic
✦ Stencil brushes, ½" diameter
✦ Stencil paper
✦ Transfer paper
✦ Metal ruler and pencil
✦ Crafts knife
✦ Rubber cement
✦ Crafts glue

Directions
Note: Cover the work surface with newspaper and plastic wrap and keep a roll of paper towels handy. Allow paints to dry thoroughly between steps. Do not heat-set paints on paper.

Stenciling: Trace the designs onto the stencil paper (see "Making Stencils," page 186). Cut out the stencil. Cover the back of the stencil paper with rubber cement. Allow to dry. Before you begin your project, practice on scrap paper as follows: Blot any excess paint

from the brush onto a paper towel. Stamp the brush in an up-and-down motion to achieve a crisp, clean edge. Working from the edges of the stencil toward the center, leave the center blank, lightly colored, or solidly colored, as desired. To prevent smears allow paints to dry and be sure the stencil is dry when you move it. When you are comfortable with your results, begin your project.

Gift Wrap: Randomly arrange the desired stencils on large sheets of paper and paint the desired motifs.

Gift Cards: Cut the paper into 10- by 7-inch pieces, then fold in half crosswise to measure 5 by 7 inches. Arrange stencils on the front of each card and paint as desired.

Tags: Cut the paper into desired sizes. Arrange the stencils and paint as desired.

Gift Bag: Using Figure 1 as a guide, make a full-sized pattern. Fold a practice piece of paper before folding the stenciled paper. (Once you have completed this bag, try making larger or smaller ones, altering the pattern as needed for the desired measurements.) Transfer the folding pattern to the wrong side of the paper. Arrange the stencils on the front and paint as desired. To score the fold lines, run a stylus over them. With wrong sides together, fold the paper at the A lines. Glue and overlap the side edges so that the A fold lines match. Allow to dry. Fold the B and C seams to the inside. At the bottom of the bag, open out the front and back sections, creasing along the D lines (Figure 2). Overlap the folded sections to form the bag bottom and glue the layers together. With right sides together, crease the E seams for the inner side seams and fold the bottom forward at F to allow the bag to fold flat.

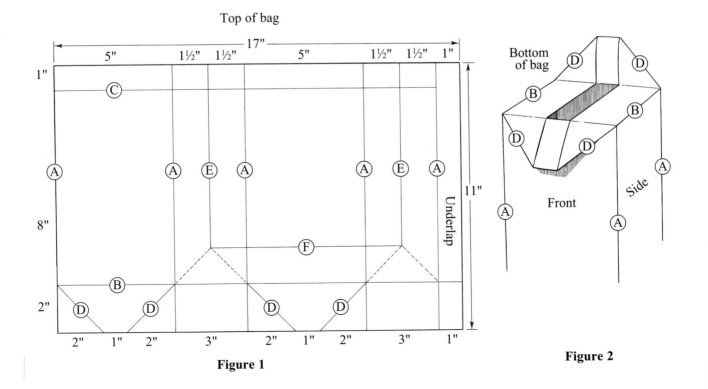

Figure 1

Figure 2

Angelic Wrappings Stencil Patterns (actual size)

Wire Mesh Vase and Votive Holders

Created by folding bronze screening around an ordinary vase and votive candle holders, this shimmering tabletop display suggests the spiritual element of Christmas and does so with contemporary flair.

Size

Vase is size desired. Votive candleholder is 2" tall.

Materials

✦ Glass votive candleholders, 2" tall
✦ Vase with narrow rim
✦ Mesh screening: bronze
✦ Thin brass wire
✦ Tin snips

Directions

Votive Holder: Using tin snips, cut an 8-inch square of screening for each votive candleholder. Fold each edge ¼ inch to the wrong side and crease the screening for the hem.

Place the screening with the hem-side down on a flat surface. Place a glass votive candleholder in the center of the screening. Beginning with the corners, bend the screening around the candleholder. Fold the excess screening to flatten it and hold it tightly around the glass. The corners of the screening should make four points. Wrap brass wire tightly around the top of the candleholder to hold the screening. Following the photograph, bend the corners gracefully outward with the tips turned down.

Vase: Cut a square of screening with sides measuring 4 times the height of the vase (for example, if the vase is 5 inches high, cut a 20-inch square). Follow the instructions for the votive candleholder, folding the mesh around the vase and wrapping the wire around the narrowest part of the vase to secure it. Pull gently outward on the corner points to stretch and shape them into petals as shown.

Shining Celestial Ornaments

Easy to make with gold paint, trims, pipe cleaners, and charms, these celestial shapes make a delightful winter window display or a welcome addition to any ornament collection.

Sizes

Ornaments are 4" to 5" in diameter.

Materials

✦ 1 sheet of illustration board
✦ Squeeze bottle of fabric paint: gold pearl
✦ Metal star, moon, and sun face charms: gold
✦ Metallic pipe cleaners: gold
✦ Assorted ribbons, trims, and rickrack: gold
✦ Spray paint: gold
✦ 8" length of cord for each ornament, ⅛" diameter: gold
✦ Tracing and transfer papers
✦ Crafts knife
✦ Hot-glue gun and glue sticks

Directions

Spray-paint the illustration board completely with gold. Allow to dry. Trace and transfer the star and sun patterns onto the illustration board (see "Transferring Patterns," page 186). Cut out the shapes with the crafts knife. Following the photograph, glue the charms in place at the center of some of the shapes. Squeezing the fabric paint directly from the bottle, paint lines and swirls on each ornament. Glue on trims and pipe cleaners as desired. Fold the 8-inch length of cord in half and knot the ends. Glue it in place at the top of each ornament for a hanging loop.

Shining Celestial Ornaments Patterns
(actual size)

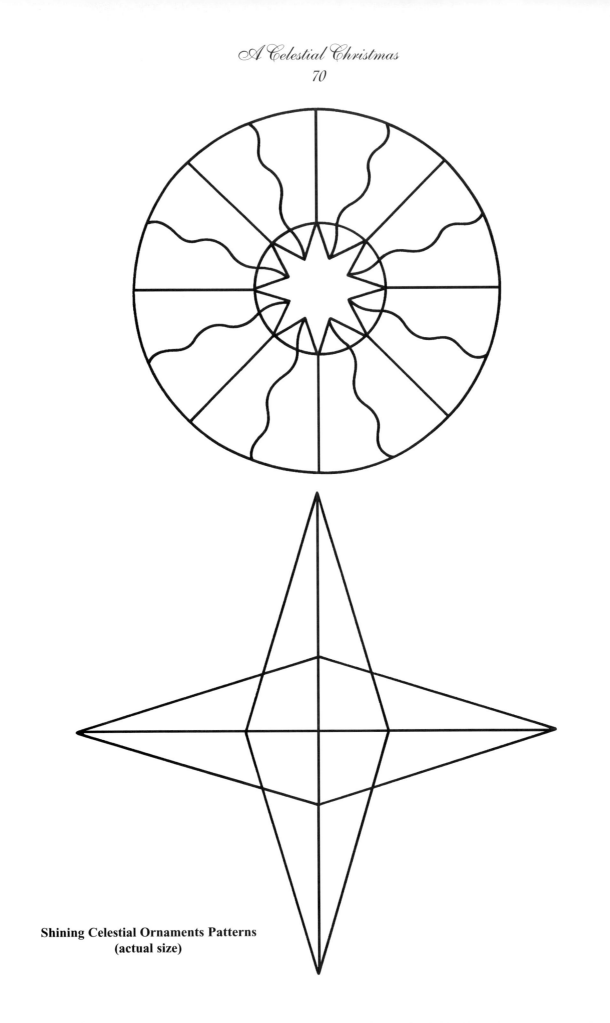

Shining Celestial Ornaments Patterns
(actual size)

To Grandmother's House We Go

Over the river and through the woods
To Grandmother's house we go.

Whether long or short, to
the country or city, a special visit to loved
ones is a long-cherished,
old-fashioned Christmas tradition that offers
a warm refuge from the chill of winter and a
chance to share the joy of the
season. A particular delight is finding familiar
Christmas treasures set out for
the occasion. The projects in this chapter are
sure to become such favorite decorations,
from a pretty painted tray to
antique-looking Victorian print ornaments.

Dutch Colonial Gingerbread House

Children always find gingerbread houses captivating. A confectionery winter wonderland lavished with sweet-treat trimmings is an almost-edible fantasy come to life. From the "slate" roof tiles to the topiary trees gracing the entryway, rich details give this quaint Dutch Colonial Gingerbread House extra charm.

Size
Gingerbread house is 10" wide × 10" tall × 7" deep.

Materials
For Each Batch of Gingerbread Dough:
- ½ cup of margarine or butter
- ½ cup of shortening
- 1 cup of sugar
- 1½ teaspoons of ground ginger
- 1½ teaspoons of ground allspice
- 1 teaspoon of baking soda
- ½ teaspoon of salt
- 1 egg
- ½ cup of molasses
- 2 tablespoons of lemon juice
- 3 cups of all-purpose flour
- 1 cup of whole-wheat flour

For Each Batch of Icing:
- 3 tablespoons of meringue powder
- 6 tablespoons of warm water
- 16 oz. of powdered sugar
- 1 teaspoon of vanilla
- ½ teaspoon of cream of tartar

For Gingerbread House Decoration:
- 2 apricot Fruit Roll-Ups®
- Marzipan
- Food coloring: green
- Life Saver Holes®
- Sliced almonds
- Silver dragées
- Gummi Savers Life Savers®
- Cinnamon dot candies
- 4 boxes Andes® mint parfaits
- Sunflower seeds
- Chocolate wafer cookies
- Peppermint candies: green and red
- Peppermint sticks: 1 green and 2 red
- Chocolate sticks
- Large and small gumdrops: green
- Large and small spearmint leaves: green

For Gingerbread Preparation and House Assembly:
- Foamcore board
- Artificial greenery
- Polyester quilt batting
- Crafts glue
- Kitchen knife, butter knife, fork, whisk, metal spatula
- Mixing bowl and electric mixer
- Wooden spoon
- Rolling pin
- Cookie sheets
- Decorating bag with tips
- Tweezers
- Ruler
- Cans for temporary supports

Directions
Gingerbread Dough: Make 2 separate batches. Do not double the recipe. Beat the margarine or butter and the shortening in a large mixing bowl until soft. Add the sugar, ginger, allspice, baking soda, and salt and mix well. Add the egg, molasses, and lemon juice and beat until mixed thoroughly. Add the flour, beating with a wooden spoon when the dough becomes too stiff for the mixer. Divide the dough in half and wrap each half in plastic wrap. Chill the dough for 3 hours or until it is firm enough to roll out.

Gingerbread: Using a floured rolling pin, roll out the dough to a ¼-inch thickness directly onto the ungreased cookie sheets. Using the ruler and the kitchen knife, cut two 10- by 6-inch pieces for the roof, two 9- by 5-inch pieces for the front and back, and one 9- by 3-inch piece for the porch roof. For each of 2 house sides, measure and cut a 7- by 9½-inch rectangle. Following Figure 1 (see page 75), measure and cut off the top triangles to form the gable.

Mark and cut out 1 window, 1½ inches wide by 2½ inches high, centered on the lower section of each house side. Mark and cut out 2 windows, 1½ inches wide by 2½ inches high, centered on the back. Mark and cut out 1 window, 1½ inches wide by 2½ inches high, on one half of the front, leaving room for the door.

Bake the pieces in a 375° oven for 10 to 12 minutes or until the edges are lightly browned. While the gingerbread pieces are still warm, remove any air bubbles with the metal spatula. Trim the pieces, if necessary. Let the pieces cool before removing them from the cookie sheets.

Icing: Make 2 separate batches. Do not double the recipe. Do not make the second batch of icing until the first batch is finished so that the icing does not dry out. Combine the meringue powder and warm water in a large mixing bowl, beating lightly with a fork. Sift the powdered sugar. Add the powdered sugar, vanilla, and cream of tartar. Beat with an electric mixer until very stiff. Use at once. Keep the icing in a bowl covered with wet paper towels to prevent it from drying out. If the icing does begin to dry out, thin it with water, a few drops at a time. If the icing separates, whisk it until blended, adding more powdered sugar to thicken it. Use firm icing to assemble and support the large house pieces and thinner icing to glue on small decorations.

House Decoration: Decorate the pieces before the house is assembled. Use the tweezers when working with smaller candies. Fill the decorating bag with thinned icing to use as glue and use the writing tip.

Unroll a Fruit Roll-Up and, from the flattened piece, cut rectangles to fit inside the windows. Use thinned icing to glue the pieces to the windows.

Roll the marzipan out to a ¹⁄₁₆-inch thickness. From the marzipan, cut 2 triangles the same measurement as the upper peaks on the sides of the house. Using the butter knife, score across the marzipan peaks for the house siding, making sure not to cut through the marzipan completely. Glue the peaks to the sides of the house. Cut 1 door, 2 by 4 inches, from the marzipan. Glue it to the front. Cut 2 shutters, ¾ by 2½ inches, for each window. Score the shutters with a knife. Glue a shutter to each side of each window. Paint the shutters with green food coloring mixed with water.

Glue Life Saver Holes around the door and below the windows. Following the photograph, glue almonds above the windows. Glue silver dragées on the almonds and on the shutter corners. Glue a Gummi Life Saver to the door for the wreath. Decorate with almonds, silver dragées, and cinnamon dots. Following the photograph, pipe lines on the windows, door, and each wall with icing.

House Assembly: Let the icing dry thoroughly between assembly steps. Use the leaf tip on the decorating bag and fill the bag with full-strength icing. Centered on the Foamcore board, draw a 7- by 9-inch rectangle to use as a baseline. Pipe a line of icing on the bottom and side edges of one side wall of the house. Pipe a line along the corresponding baseline and position the side piece. Support the side with cans or clay. Repeat to position the front, back, and other side, pressing the pieces together at the corners. When the icing is dry, remove any cans and add extra icing to support the pieces as necessary.

Pipe a thick line of icing along the roof lines and across the top edges of the house. Position the roof pieces and press the pieces together. Working with one small portion at a time, spread the roof with icing and place the mint parfait candies flat side down, staggering them like shingles and cutting them to fit at the edges. Press them in place. In the same manner, cover the porch roof with mint parfaits. Trim the edges of the roof pieces with sunflower seeds and cinnamon dots.

For the chimney, glue the wide surfaces of 2 chocolate wafers together, then glue a wafer to each side edge (Figure 2). Cut one end to the same angle as the roof pitch and glue in place. For the porch floor, separate wafers into halves, removing the center icing if you wish, and glue them flat, side by side, along the front of the house.

For a porch column, stack and glue 2 peppermints together, then glue a Gummi Life Saver to the top of the peppermints. Insert a peppermint stick in the hole and glue another peppermint to the other end of the peppermint stick. Make 1 green and 2 red columns. Following the photograph, space the columns evenly along the house front and glue them in place. Glue the porch roof to the columns and to the seam of the roof and the front, propping it until the icing dries.

Cover the Foamcore board with the batting for snow and glue it in place with crafts glue. Separate the wafers and use icing to glue them in place for the walkway. Following the photograph, glue the chocolate sticks together to make a fence and glue it in place. Arrange and position the gumdrops and spearmint leaves for bushes as desired. Thin the icing and drip it off a spoon onto the bushes and the fence for snow. Arrange the greenery around the edges of the Foamcore board and glue in place with crafts glue.

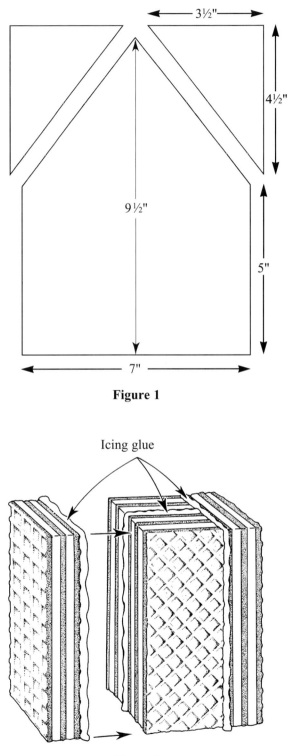

Figure 1

Icing glue

Figure 2

Painted Tray

*The whimsical folk art style of this
Painted Tray adds extra charm
to its enchanting winter scene.
Whether in early December or on Christmas
Eve, bringing home the tree is
always a merry and much-anticipated event.*

Size
Tray is 16" × 21".

Materials
+ 16" × 21" wooden tray
+ Acrylic paint: blue, gold, pink, white, black, red, forest green, dark red, moss green, mushroom, and slate blue
+ Foam paintbrushes, 1" and 2" wide
+ Round-point paintbrush, #4
+ Shader paintbrushes, ¼" and ½" wide
+ Script (very fine) paintbrush
+ Silver leaf and gold-leaf adhesive (or use metallic silver paint)
+ Fine and medium sandpaper and tack cloth
+ Natural sponge
+ Tracing and transfer papers
+ Spray sealer

Directions
Cover the work surface with newspaper and plastic wrap and keep a roll of paper towels handy. Allow paints to dry thoroughly between steps.

Tray: Sand the tray with the medium sandpaper, then the fine; wipe with the tack cloth. Using the wider foam brush, paint the tray slate blue. Cover the inner and outer sides of the tray with the gold-leaf adhesive. Apply the silver leaf, smoothing it in place with your finger. Patch areas with small pieces of leaf until all the sides are completely covered.

Design: Enlarge the pattern and transfer the basic shapes onto the center of the tray (see "Enlarging Patterns" and "Transferring Patterns," pages 185 and 186). Follow the pattern and the photograph for finer details as you work. Leaving the center of the tray clear, cover the silver sides with paper to keep them clean while painting.

Following the photograph and using the 1-inch foam brush, paint the horizon of the sky pink. Wipe with a damp paper towel to streak the sky. Paint the snow areas. Using the small shader brush, paint the houses and the church. Mix moss green, mushroom, and dark red to make the tree trunk color; then paint the tree trunks. Using the script brush, paint fine branches with the mixed color.

Details: Following the photograph and using the shader and script brushes, paint the people, house details, and sleigh. Mix white with pink and gold to use as a flesh color. Mix mushroom with white to paint shadows. Mix forest green with a little white and use the round brush to make half-moon shapes for the evergreen branches. Paint white on the roofs of the houses and on the evergreen trees for snow.

Use the fine brush to paint the fine details. With white, paint dots for snowflakes. Thin the white with water, then use the sponge to apply thinned paint lightly over the snow areas. Allow to dry overnight. Spray the entire tray with 2 coats of sealer.

1 square = 1 inch

Painted Tray Pattern

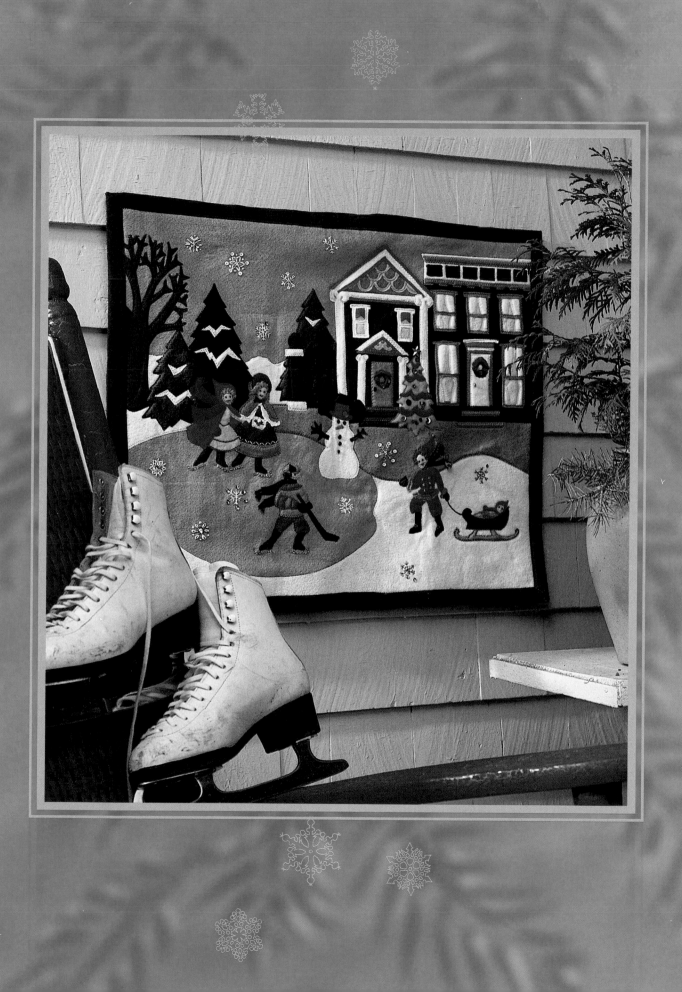

Skating Party Banner

Evoking an essential element of winter in the Victorian era, a lively skating party scene is richly depicted in felt appliqué. Display this colorful banner and it may inspire a present-day ice-skating outing complete with hot cocoa.

Size
Banner is 20½" × 25".

Materials
- 1 yd. of felt: sky blue
- ½ yd. of felt: royal blue
- ¼ yd. each of felt: white and forest green
- 9" × 12" block of each felt: red, Kelly green, apple green, rose pink, light pink, lavender, purple, black, gray, dark brown, light brown, gold, champagne, beige, orange, and yellow-orange
- 1 skein each of 6-strand embroidery floss: white, black, red, gold, green, blue, and dark green or colors to match felt
- 1 skein of metallic thread: silver
- ¼ yd. of satin ribbon, ¼" wide: red
- 5 yd. of paper-backed fusible web
- Matching threads
- Embroidery needles
- 1 small star button, ⅝" diameter: gold
- Assorted sequins: white, silver, and assorted colors
- 2 small curtain rings for hanging
- Dressmaker's pencil
- Tracing paper
- Crafts glue

Directions

Preparation: Before you begin your project, please read "Enlarging Patterns" and "Transferring Designs," pages 185 and 186. Enlarge the pattern. From sky blue, cut out two 20½- by 25-inch pieces for banner front and back. Trace the outline for each appliqué piece and transfer onto the paper side of the fusible web. Following the photograph for colors and the manufacturer's instructions, fuse the web to the wrong side of the appropriate-color felt. Note that the fine details, such as the snowflakes and the faces, are to be embroidered later. Small circles on the pattern indicate sequins to be added later. Cut out the appliqué shapes, adding small underlap edges on shapes when necessary so that the background fabric won't show (Figure 1). You need not cut away the underlying layer for very small or narrow shapes. From royal blue, cut two 2- by 20½-inch strips for the side borders and two 2- by 25-inch strips for the top and bottom borders.

Appliqué: Beginning with the larger background shapes, remove the paper backing, arrange the pieces on the banner front, and fuse them in place. Fuse one area at a time until all shapes are in place. Using a narrow zigzag stitch and matching threads, sew around all of the pieces. Hand-sew the smaller shapes. Using the dressmaker's pencil, transfer

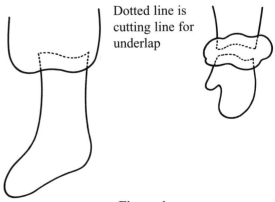

Dotted line is cutting line for underlap

Figure 1

Skating Party Banner Pattern

the embroidered details to banner front. Using 6 strands of floss and the desired embroidery stitches (see "Embroidery Stitches," page 188), embroider the details. Work the skate blades with 4 strands of silver thread.

Assembly: With wrong sides together, pin the front and back of the banner together. Fold a side border in half lengthwise. Slide one side edge of the banner between the open edges of the border; pin in place. Fold the remaining side, top, and bottom borders over their respective edges and pin them in place.

Leaving a small overlap, cut the corners at an angle to miter them. Using a narrow zigzag stitch and matching thread, sew around the borders and miters.

Sew the curtain rings to the top corners on the back of the banner. Glue the sequins on the snowflakes, wreath, snowman, and Christmas tree decorations. Cut the ribbon into 2 pieces; tie a small knot at the center of each piece and trim the ends. Glue in place for the wreath ribbons. Sew or glue the star button to the top of the decorated tree.

Victorian Print Ornaments

*Photocopies of antique etchings are
delicately painted and festively trimmed to create
old-fashioned Victorian Print Ornaments.
They are charming when hung from a swag or
garland; or use the same technique to create ornate
Christmas cards and tags for packages.*

Size
Ornament size depends on the size
of the print used.

Materials
✦ Illustration prints from *Old-fashioned Christmas in Illustration and Decoration* and *Handbook of Early Advertising Art, Pictorial Volume*, both by Clarence P. Hormung from Dover Press, or desired prints
✦ 1 sheet of Foamcore™ board, ⅛" thick
✦ 1 pad of parchment paper, 8½" × 11"
✦ Glitter pens: red, blue, and green
✦ Watercolor paints and paintbrush
✦ 8" length of ribbon for each ornament hanger, ⅛" wide (or use pipe cleaners)
✦ Assorted ribbons, trims, and rickrack as desired
✦ Pony beads, ¼": red
✦ Sticker stars
✦ Metallic pipe cleaners: gold
✦ Spray adhesive
✦ Crafts knife
✦ Crafts glue
✦ Pencil and ruler

Directions
Preparation: The prints we used for this project are reproduced on pages 84 to 86. You can photocopy them directly from the book if you wish, adjusting the sizes as desired. Using sheets of parchment paper in a copy machine, copy the chosen design(s), reducing or enlarging as desired and leaving 2 inches between the motifs if copying several onto one sheet.

From *Old-fashioned Christmas in Illustration and Decoration* we used "Doll" and "Drum," each enlarged 125 percent; "Santa Claus with Pipe," reduced to 60 percent of original size; and "Two Children Carrying Tree," reduced to 90 percent of original size. From *Handbook of Early Advertising Art, Pictorial Volume*, we used "Santa in the Circle of Holly," actual size.

Ornament: Using a pencil and a ruler, draw a rectangle around each motif, adding ¾ inch all around to allow room for the trims to be glued onto the motif edges. Cut out the rectangle. Measure and mark a piece of Foamcore the same size as the rectangle. Spray the wrong side of paper with adhesive and attach to the Foamcore board, smoothing out any wrinkles with the palm of your hand.

Referring to the photo, paint with watercolors as desired. Allow to dry. Use the glitter pens to paint the background, decorations, and borders as desired. Allow to dry. Glue trims around the motif edges. Glue pipe cleaners around the ornament edges. Add sticker stars as desired.

Make hanging loops for the ornaments by either of the following methods. Fold 8 inches of ribbon in half and thread the folded end through a pony bead. Knot the end of the ribbon above the bead to secure it, then glue the bead in place just below the knot. Glue the cut ends of the ribbon to the backs of some ornaments. For other ornaments, cut two 5-inch lengths from a metallic pipe cleaner; thread an end of each through a pony bead. Twist the ends together and glue the bead in place just below the twists. Spread the ends of the pipe cleaners and glue an end to each top corner on the back of the ornament.

Victorian Print Ornaments Design

Victorian Print Ornaments Design

Victorian Print Ornaments Designs

Dowel Pyramid Tree

Constructing a pyramid tree was a Christmastime custom in Germany even before that of bringing in an evergreen to decorate. Each level spotlights favorite Christmas trinkets and treasures. Early German examples, sometimes lit by candles, very often included a crèche and angels.

Size
Pyramid tree is 24" tall.

Materials
✦ Foamcore board: green
✦ 13" of wooden dowel, 5⁄16" diameter
✦ 4 yd. of decorative trim, ¼" wide: red/green/gold
✦ Foil doily, 8" diameter: gold
✦ Acrylic paint: green
✦ 6 pencil Santa ornaments, 6" tall

- Miniature Christmas tree, 6" tall, including base
- 3 miniature Christmas trees, 2" tall, including base
- Assorted angels and charms
- Assorted Christmas decorations and ornaments
- Assorted dollhouse Christmas presents and tree decorations
- Miniature crèche
- Artificial fruits, berries, flowers, pinecones, and holly leaves
- Sponge
- Yardstick
- Crafts knife
- Hot-glue gun and glue sticks
- Protractor or 60°-angle triangle (optional)
- Tall cans or stacks of books for support

Directions

Triangles: Following Figure 1 and using the yardstick, mark onto wrong side of Foamcore board 1 equilateral triangle (all sides equal) in each of the 4 following sizes: 6-inch base and $5\frac{3}{16}$-inch height; 9-inch base and $7\frac{13}{16}$-inch height; 12-inch base and $10\frac{7}{16}$-inch height; and 15-inch base and $13\frac{5}{16}$-inch height. Measure carefully (slanted sides should measure the same as the base), so the pyramid will stack up correctly. Cut out triangles, using the crafts knife to make clean cuts. Stack triangles, centered, on top of one another and lightly mark the next smaller triangle on the right side of each of the 3 largest triangles.

Mark ¾ inch inside the line at each corner for placing the dowels and pencil Santas. Mark ¾ inch in from each corner on wrong side of the 9- and 12-inch triangles. Glue trim around edges of each triangle, overlapping the ends.

Supports: Using the sponge, paint the dowel green. Allow it to dry. Cut three 4-inch lengths of the dowel. Glue a 4-inch length of trim down the length of each dowel. Glue one end of each dowel onto wrong side of smallest tri-

angle at corners. Cut off the hangers of ornaments and pencil Santas, if necessary. Glue heads of Santas onto wrong side of 9- and 12-inch triangles where marked. Center and stack triangles to ensure that the mark for placing the dowels and Santas on the lower triangles is correct, remarking if needed (this helps in placing the decorations). Unstack triangles. Rest each on a tall can to support it. Keep the surface flat as you decorate it.

Decorations: Following the photograph and leaving the marked spaces for the dowels clear, decorate each triangle with the assorted decorations, crèche, fruits, and leaves as follows: Glue the doily in place on the 15-inch triangle. Arrange and glue the fruits, flowers, leaves, and berries on the doily. Position the holly leaves and berries or pinecones at each corner near the Santa marks and glue them in place. Glue the angels and ornaments in place on the 12-inch triangle. Glue the crèche in the center of the 9-inch triangle. Glue the miniature trees in each corner. Decorate the 6-inch Christmas tree as desired and glue it in place on the center of the smallest triangle. Glue presents under the tree. Beginning from the bottom, stack the decorated triangles and glue bottoms of Santas and dowels in place.

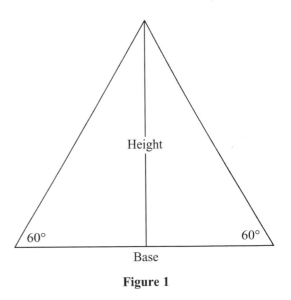

Figure 1

Happy Holidays Sampler

Reminiscent of early-nineteenth-century designs, this cross-stitch sampler features an inviting brick house, frolicking dogs, reindeer, and angels heralding the Christmas message, all in classic colors and simple designs.

Size

Embroidered design area is 9¼" × 13"

Materials

✦ 13" × 16" piece of 14-count Aida fabric: khaki
✦ 1 skein each of 6-strand embroidery floss (see key for colors)
✦ Contrasting thread
✦ Embroidery hoop and tapestry needle
✦ Frame (optional; see Note below)

Directions

Cross-stitching: See "How to Cross-stitch" and "Embroidery Stitches," pages 187 and 188. With contrasting basting thread, mark the horizontal and vertical centers of the fabric. Center the cross-stitch design on the Aida fabric, matching the fabric center with the arrows on the chart. Following the chart and key, embroider the design. Work cross-stitches with 2 strands of floss. Work backstitches, French knots, and straight stitches with 2 strands of floss. After the embroidery is finished, carefully remove the basting stitches and gently hand-wash the fabric in cold water. Dry it flat and press it on the wrong side.

Note: If you would like an heirloom-quality cross-stitch project, we recommend taking the completed, pressed piece to a professional framer who has had experience framing needlework. You've already invested your time; it's worth protecting that investment!

Center

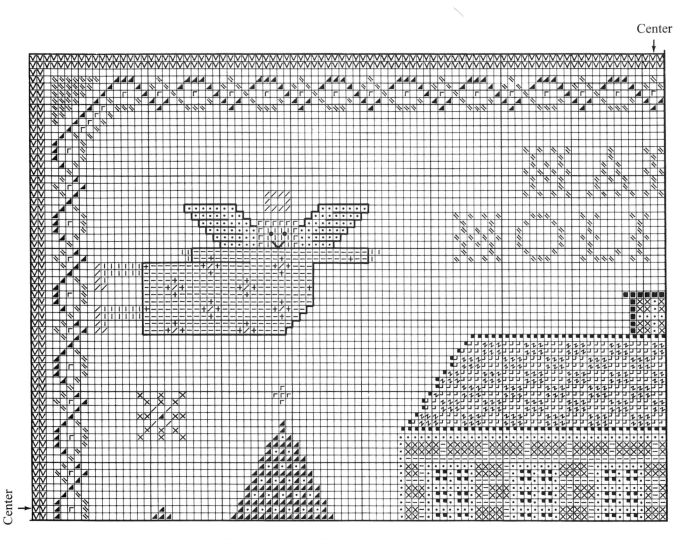

Center

Happy Holidays Sampler (top left section)

Anchor		DMC	KEY Color
387	•	Ecru	Ecru
778	—	3774	Sportsman Flesh Very Light
1009	I	3770	Flesh Very Light
43	⧅	815	Garnet Medium
340	✕	919	Red Copper
9046	V	321	Christmas Red
218	◢	890	Pistachio Ultra Dark
907	/	832	Golden Olive
214	ͻ	368	Pistachio Light
264	O	3348	Yellow Green Light

Overlap from adjacent section

Center

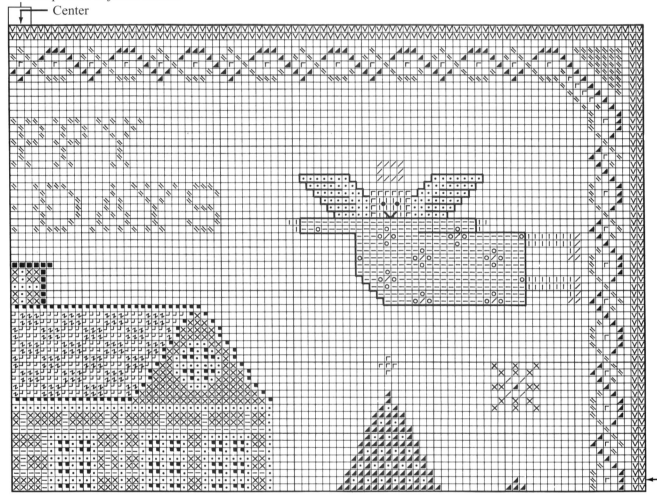

Center

Happy Holidays Sampler (top right section)

Anchor		DMC	Color
305	Γ	725	Topaz
401	■	413	Pewter Gray Dark
399	↗	318	Steel Gray Light
234	⌐	762	Pearl Gray Very Light
360	■	898	Coffee Brown Very Dark
379	+	840	Beige Brown Medium

Anchor		DMC	Color
			BACKSTITCH
9046	⌐	321	Christmas Red, angels' mouths
360	⌐	898	Coffee Brown Very Dark, angels' gowns and wings, antlers
			FRENCH KNOT
387	●	Ecru	Ecru, dogs' eyes
218	●	890	Pistachio Ultra Dark, angels' eyes
360	●	898	Coffee Brown Very Dark, deer's eye

Anchor	DMC	KEY	
		Color	
387	•	Ecru	Ecru
778	—	3774	Sportsman Flesh Very Light
1009	│	3770	Flesh Very Light
43	╲	815	Garnet Medium
340	✕	919	Red Copper
9046	V	321	Christmas Red
218	◣	890	Pistachio Ultra Dark
907	╱	832	Golden Olive
214	ς	368	Pistachio Light
264	○	3348	Yellow Green Light

Happy Holidays Sampler (lower right section)

Center

Overlap from adjacent section

Happy Holidays Sampler (lower left section)

Center

Overlap from adjacent section

Anchor		DMC	Color
305	⌐	725	Topaz
401	■	413	Pewter Gray Dark
399	◹	318	Steel Gray Light
234	⊔	762	Pearl Gray Very Light
360	■	898	Coffee Brown Very Dark
379	+	840	Beige Brown Medium

Anchor		DMC	Color
			BACKSTITCH
9046	⌐	321	Christmas Red, angels' mouths
360	⌐	898	Coffee Brown Very Dark, angels' gowns and wings, antlers
			FRENCH KNOT
387	●	Ecru	Ecru, dogs' eyes
218	●	890	Pistachio Ultra Dark, angels' eyes
360	●	898	Coffee Brown Very Dark, deer's eye

A Child's Christmas

The children were nestled all snug in their beds,
While visions of sugar-plums
danced in their heads...

It has been said that Christmas is for
children most of all. Indeed, their delight during
this season reflects the magic of the holiday.
Their involvement in preparations and gift giving
adds to their fun and anticipation, and they
learn to appreciate the spiritual and historical
aspects of Christmas. Holiday time spent with
young ones will furnish the memories they
(and you!) will later cherish—and you may even
find yourself reexperiencing the wonder of
Christmas through their eyes.

Christmas Toy Box

A plain wooden planter is transformed into a charming toy box (or even a holder for a small Christmas tree) hand-painted with colorful scenes—an angel, a Christmas tree, a snowman, and a fat, contented cat—making this a possible year-round item for a child's room.

Size
Box is 13" square.

Materials
✦ 13" square planter box
✦ 8 wooden balls with one flat side, 3" diameter
✦ Acrylic paint: gold (A), yellow (B), peach (C), royal blue (D), clay (E), orange (F), green (G), red (H), light blue (I), white (J), black (K), metallic antique gold (L), and gray (M)
✦ Paintbrushes: round-point #4 and fine
✦ Foam paintbrush, 1" wide
✦ Fine and medium sandpaper and tack cloth
✦ Wood glue
✦ Polyurethane
✦ Tracing and transfer papers

Directions
Note: Cover the work surface with newspaper and plastic wrap. Allow paints to dry thoroughly between steps.

Box: Sand the planter with medium sandpaper, then with fine. Wipe with the tack cloth. Following the photograph, glue the flat side of the wooden balls in place on the top and bottom corners of the box. Allow to dry. Using the foam paintbrush, paint the side panels of the box light blue. Paint the corner side trims green. Paint the top trim and the wooden balls red.

Designs: Enlarge and transfer the designs to the centers of the side panels (see "Enlarging Patterns" and "Transferring Patterns," pages 185 and 186). Following the photographs and using the round-pointed paintbrush, paint the designs. Paint the large areas first, then fill in the details, painting fine detail lines on each panel with the fine paintbrush. When you are working over other colors, the paints may need 2 coats. Using gold, paint wavy lines along the top and corner trims. Allow to dry for 24 hours. Paint with 2 coats of polyurethane.

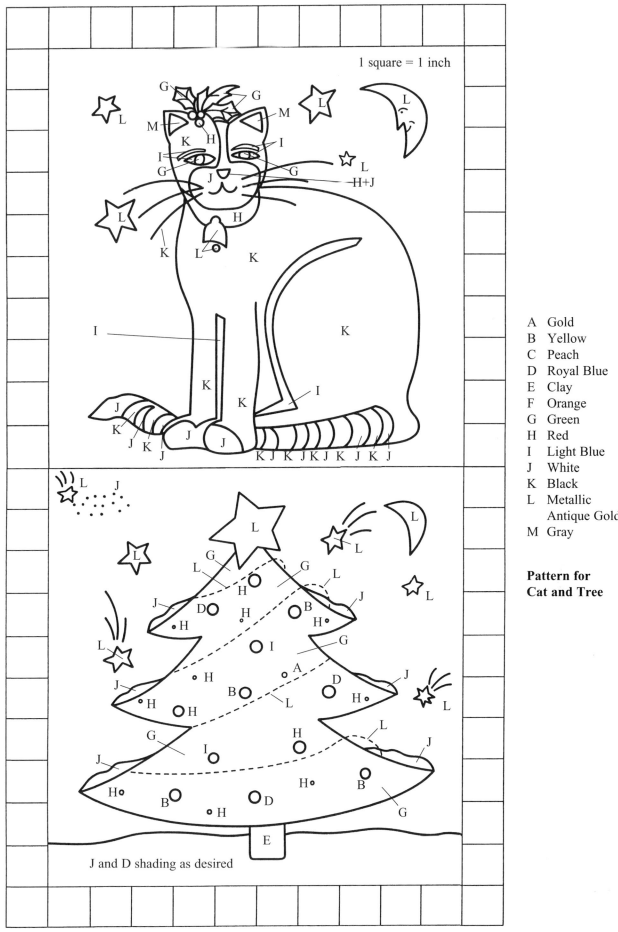

1 square = 1 inch

A Gold
B Yellow
C Peach
D Royal Blue
E Clay
F Orange
G Green
H Red
I Light Blue
J White
K Black
L Metallic
   Antique Gold
M Gray

**Pattern for
Cat and Tree**

J and D shading as desired

1 square = 1 inch

K

L ☆   ☆ L

L ☆

H   E

K
J   E   K
K
G   H

G   A

K ○
K ○   J
K ○

J

J and D
shading as desired

A   Gold
B   Yellow
C   Peach
D   Royal Blue
E   Clay
F   Orange
G   Green
H   Red
I   Light Blue
J   White
K   Black
L   Metallic
    Antique Gold
M   Gray

**Pattern for
Snowman
and Angel**

L ☆   ☆ L

F
E
L
C
J   L

B+J

L   L
L   L
J+L   C   L   C   J+L
L   L

B+J

L

J and D
shading as
desired

L

Foil Star
Ornaments

*This easy, no-mess project is a wonderful
way for children to create delightful decorations
for the tree. Cut from foil origami paper,
they look great as individual Foil Star
Ornaments or hung in twos or threes; or
connect several to make colorful garlands.*

Size

Stars are 2" to 2⅞" wide; ornaments are lengths desired.

Materials

✦ 6" squares of foil origami paper: assorted colors
✦ Metallic pipe cleaners: assorted colors
✦ Paper punch
✦ Tracing paper
✦ Glue stick

Directions

Use the glue stick to cover the backs of 2 different-color sheets of foil paper. Line up the edges and press the backs of the sheets together, smoothing them out to remove air bubbles. Trace the star shapes and cut them out for patterns. Draw the star shape on the paper with a pen. Cut out the stars. Punch a hole in the top and bottom of each star to string the stars together, but punch only one hole in the bottom star.

Cut the pipe cleaners into 3-inch lengths. Thread the pipe cleaner through the top hole of one star and the bottom hole of another and twist the ends together. String the stars together as desired. For hanging, insert one end of a pipe cleaner through the top hole. Fold up this end ½ inch and twist it around the pipe cleaner to secure. Fold the opposite end of the pipe cleaner to make a hook shape.

Foil Star Ornaments Patterns
(actual size)

Popcorn Cones

*Projects with edible elements are always fun
and seem to attract young volunteers like magic!
These Popcorn Cone ornaments are simple to
make but are fragile, so handle with care.*

Size

Ornaments are 6" long.

Materials

+ Sugar ice cream cones
+ Popcorn
+ 8" length of ribbon for each cone, ³⁄₈"
wide: red and white polka dot
+ 1 ribbon rose bow for each cone: red and
white check
+ Low-temperature glue gun and glue sticks

Directions

Fill the cone with popcorn until it is almost
full. Cover the top of the popcorn with a layer
of glue. Glue on another layer of the popcorn
to form a rounded top. Glue one end of the 8-
inch length of ribbon to each side of the cone
for hanging. Glue the ribbon rose bow to the
cone 1 inch below the edge and centered
between the ribbon ends. Completed ornaments are not edible.

Wooden Blocks

*The antique, delicate appearance of these
decoupage Wooden Blocks is deceptive.
They are tough enough to play with today and
pass down to future generations. Any cutout wrapping paper motifs will look wonderful, from ani-
mals or letters to cars or Christmas trees.*

Sizes

Blocks are 4" and 6" cubes.

Materials

+ Solid pine posts, 4" and 6" square
+ Acrylic gloss enamel paint: forest green
and burgundy
+ Acrylic paint: metallic gold
+ Decoupage finish or acrylic gel medium
+ Two foam paintbrushes, 1" wide
+ Sponge
+ Wrapping paper in assorted Christmas
patterns
+ Saw
+ Router (optional)
+ Fine and medium sandpaper and tack cloth
+ Small, sharp scissors (e.g., cuticle or
embroidery)
+ Spray sealer
+ Clean rag

Directions

Preparation: Measure and cut the posts into
square blocks. Rout the edges to round them
slightly, or round them off with medium sandpaper. With fine sandpaper, sand the edges
smooth. Wipe with the tack cloth. Paint the
blocks forest green or burgundy. Allow to dry.
With the sponge and gold paint, gild the block
edges and sides. With a clean rag rub off most
of the paint on the side surfaces, leaving only
a dusting of gold. Allow to dry.

Decoupage: Using the small, sharp scissors,
cut out the desired images. Paint the back of
the cutout with decoupage finish or acrylic gel
medium and position it on the block. Rub the
image with your finger to secure it and to
remove any air bubbles. Attach a cutout to
each remaining side of each block. Let the
blocks dry thoroughly. Spray with 2 coats of
sealer.

Topiary Bear

*Something about the friendly face of a
teddy bear makes him a favorite with children.
This moss-covered Topiary Bear would
be welcome in a child's room or a front entrance,
happily greeting visitors of all ages.*

Size
Topiary is 13" tall.

Materials
✦ 4 floral foam blocks, 3" × 4" × 8"
✦ Plastic foam balls, 1 each in 5", 4", 3", and
2" diameter
✦ 1½ yd. wire-edged ribbon, 1½" wide:
plaid

✦ Green sheet moss
✦ 2 artificial holly leaves
✦ 3 red berries
✦ 2 crystal doll eyes, 18 mm
✦ Teddy bear nose: black
✦ Pipe cleaner: black
✦ Toothpicks
✦ Serrated knife
✦ Hot-glue gun and glue sticks

Directions
Use toothpicks throughout to connect the
pieces. Half the length of the toothpick should
be inserted into each of the pieces. Trim the
toothpick if needed to keep the ends from pro-
truding through the surface of the foam.

Body: Use 1 floral block for the trunk of the body. Cut the 4-inch-diameter plastic foam ball in half with the serrated knife. On the flat side of each half of the 4-inch ball, insert toothpicks all around, close to the edge. Following the diagram (Figure 1), position and secure both ball halves on the trunk for the stomach.

Head: To make the head, cut ⅓ from the 5-inch-diameter ball. Insert toothpicks on flat side of the 5-inch ball, then position and secure it on top of the trunk. Insert toothpicks on flat side of the remaining third of the 5-inch ball. Position and secure it in place on the head for the snout, scraping out and shaping the flat side to fit the curve of the head ball. Cut the 3-inch-diameter ball in thirds. Reserve the middle third. To make the ears, scrape and shape the edge of the 2 outer (rounded) thirds of the 3-inch ball to fit securely on either side of the head. Insert toothpicks along the shaped edge and secure the ears in place.

Limbs: From each of 2 floral blocks, cut a leg piece 3 by 3 by 7½ inches. Measure and mark 4 inches along one long edge of each piece. Following the leg cutting diagram in Figure 1, draw a diagonal line from the 4-inch mark to the end of the opposite long edge and cut off the end along the line. Insert toothpicks along the angled cut edge and secure one piece on each side of the lower trunk for the legs. Cut the 2-inch-diameter ball into thirds. To make the feet, insert toothpicks on the flat side of the 2 outer (rounded) thirds of the 2-inch ball. Secure them on top of outer edge of legs.

From the last floral block, cut 2 arm pieces 2 by 2 by 6 inches. Measure and mark 3½ inches along one long edge of each piece (see Figure 1). Draw a diagonal line from the 3½-inch mark to the end of the opposite long edge and cut off the end along the line. Insert toothpicks along the angled cut edge and secure one piece on each side of the body for arms.

Trims: Shape the bear to have fairly smooth curved surfaces, trimming off corners and filling in empty spaces with reserved scraps of foam. Cover the topiary bear completely with sheet moss and hot-glue it in place. Poke your finger gently into the foam to mark the placement of the eyes and the nose. Glue the eyes and the nose in place. For mouth, cut two 1¼-inch lengths of the pipe cleaner. Curve each piece slightly and glue it in place below the nose. Tie the ribbon around the neck in a bow. Trim the ends and bend the bow and ends as desired. Glue the red berries and holly leaves in place just below the bow.

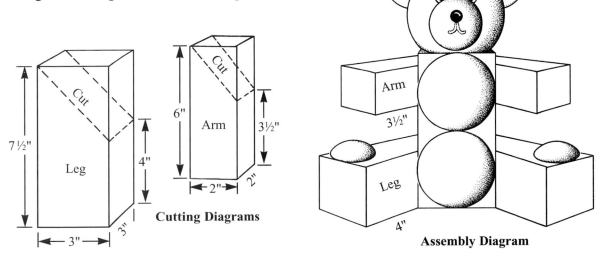

Cutting Diagrams

Assembly Diagram

Figure 1

Topsy-Turvy Doll

A treasured toy for generations,
a Topsy-Turvy Doll is twice the fun!
Flip the skirt and the little girl
becomes a friendly feline. This country
cat and girl duo will bring a smile of
delight and years of cuddling to their
lucky owner.

Size
Complete doll is 12" tall.

Materials
✦ ¼ yd. of unbleached muslin
✦ ⅝ yd. of plaid fabric for cat's clothes: red
✦ ⅝ yd. of print fabric for girl's clothes: red
✦ 1 yd. of medium rickrack: red
✦ 1½ yd. of narrow lace trim: white
✦ 1 yd. of twine
✦ Small amounts of embroidery floss: brown, rose, blue, and red
✦ Matching sewing threads
✦ Polyester stuffing
✦ Embroidery needle and hoop
✦ 2 small buttons
✦ Embroidered handkerchief, about 10" square
✦ Curly wool doll hair: auburn
✦ Dressmaker's pencil and dressmaker's carbon
✦ Tracing paper
✦ Cosmetic blush and cotton swab

Directions
Note: Before you begin your project, please read "Dyeing with Tea," page 187; "Enlarging Patterns," page 185; "Transferring Patterns," page 186; and "Embroidery Stitches," page 188. For all seams place fabric pieces right sides together and make ¼-inch seams (unless otherwise indicated).

Preparation: Cut the muslin in half to make two 9- by 22½-inch pieces. Tea-dye one piece. Enlarge the cat and girl half-patterns and transfer 2 complete cat body patterns onto the tea-dyed muslin. Transfer 2 complete girl body patterns onto the undyed muslin. Do not cut out the pieces yet. Transfer the facial features onto the front of one cat piece and one girl piece. Using the embroidery hoop, needle, and floss, embroider the facial features. On the cat's face, use 4 strands of brown floss to work the eyes in French knots, wrapping around the needle twice. Work the nose in satin stitch and the mouth in stem stitch. On the girl's face, use 3 strands of floss to work the blue eyes in satin stitch, the red mouth in stem stitch, and the rose nose in backstitch. Cut out the pattern pieces.

Assembly: Use matching thread and tiny stitches to sew the cat body pieces together, leaving the lower edge open. In the same manner, sew around the girl's body. Trim the seams; clip the corners and curves. Turn right side out and press. Topstitch across the base of each of the cat's ears. Stuff the heads and the arms, using a chopstick or stuffing tool to fill the arms. Topstitch across each arm at the shoulder seams on each doll. Finish stuffing, leaving 1 inch at the lower edge of each doll unstuffed. Turn under ½ inch around the lower edge of the cat's body. Insert the lower edge of the girl's body ½ inch into the cat's body and slipstitch the bodies together, adding stuffing if necessary. Using the cotton swab, apply a small amount of cosmetic blush to the cheeks of the girl and the cat. Hand-sew the doll hair securely around the girl's head.

Bodice: Trace the bodice pattern. Cut one 8¾-by 33½-inch piece from each red print fabric and reserve for the skirts. Fold the remaining fabric in half and with the indicated edge along the fold, transfer and cut 1 bodice from each red fabric. Cut a slit along the folded edge where indicated for the neck. Fold and press ¼ inch to the wrong side around the neck edge and along the cuff of each sleeve. Topstitch lace trim along each sleeve cuff of the girl's bodice. Sew the side and sleeve seams of each bodice. Using 3 strands of red embroidery floss and running stitches, gather the sleeve cuffs. In same manner, gather the neck edge. Slip the print bodice onto the girl and the plaid bodice onto the cat. Pull up the gathers to fit the arms and the neck, and knot the thread to secure.

Skirt: Holding both skirt fabrics with right sides together, sew along one long edge of the skirts. Open out the joined skirt piece. Fold the skirt unit in half crosswise and sew the short edges together for the back seam, forming a tube. Turn up the bottom half of the tube so that the wrong sides of the skirts are together and the long seam is at the lower edge. Sew lace trim along the lower edge of the print side of the skirt. Position and hand-sew red rick-rack along the lower edge of the plaid side of the skirt, covering the stitching line of the lace.

Turn under ¼ inch along the top edge of each skirt. Using 3 strands of red embroidery floss and running stitches, gather the top edge of each skirt separately. Position the skirts on the doll, pull the threads, and knot to secure around the waists of both the cat and the girl.

The waistline for each is about 2 inches away from the body joining.

Wrap twine from the back to the front around the cat's waist; crossing the pieces on the chest, take one end over each shoulder, cross in the back, and bring to the front around the waist. Tie into a bow and trim the ends.

Girl's Apron: Cut the handkerchief in half. Gather the raw edge of the embroidered half for the apron skirt. Pull up the gathers to measure 4½ inches, marking the center of the gathered edge. From the remaining handkerchief, cut a 1- by 6-inch strip for the neck strap, a 1- by 12-inch strip for the waistband (piecing strip for the proper length), and a 1¼- by 2½-inch piece for the bib. Turn under ¼ inch along the long edges of each strip and press. Turn under ¼ inch along one long edge and both short edges of the bib; press. Topstitch the pressed edges of bib and neck strap if desired.

Fold the waistband in half lengthwise with wrong sides together. Mark the center of the waistband strip. Insert the gathered edge of the apron skirt between the open edges of the strip, matching the centers. Topstitch the open edges of the strip together, sewing the apron skirt in place at the center. With right sides facing up, matching the centers, cover the unhemmed bottom ¼ inch of the bib with the waistband; topstitch the waistband to the bib. Tie the apron around the girl's waist. Wrap the neck strap around the girl's neck with the ends tucked under the corners of the bib. Sew a button to each bib corner, attaching the strap end as you sew.

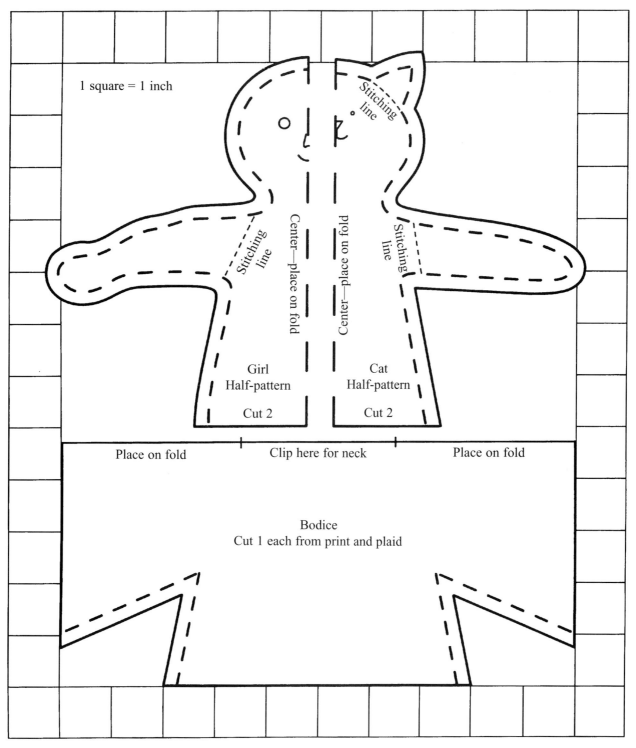

1 square = 1 inch

Stitching line

Stitching line

Center—place on fold

Center—place on fold

Stitching line

Stitching line

Girl
Half-pattern

Cut 2

Cat
Half-pattern

Cut 2

Place on fold

Clip here for neck

Place on fold

Bodice
Cut 1 each from print and plaid

Topsy-Turvy Doll Patterns

Nutcracker Stocking

Delight a child with this felt appliquéd Nutcracker Stocking; it is certain to be filled with lots of treats and wrapped surprises year after year.

Size
Stocking is 14" tall.

Materials
+ ½ yd. each of felt: dark green and red
+ 9" × 12" block each of felt: white, bright blue, yellow orange, black, gray, light pink, and hot pink
+ 1 yd. of paper-backed fusible web
+ Black and matching threads
+ 1 skein of rug yarn: red
+ 2 tiny pompoms: pink
+ 3 black seed beads
+ Tracing paper and transfer paper
+ Crafts glue

Directions
Preparation: Before you begin your project, please read "Enlarging Patterns" and "Transferring Patterns," pages 185 and 186. Enlarge the pattern, then transfer patterns for each separate appliqué piece onto the paper backing of the fusible web and rough-cut them out. Following the photograph for colors, fuse the web to the wrong side of the felt. Cut out appliqué shapes, adding small underlap edges on shapes when necessary, so that the background fabric won't show through (Figure 1). You need not cut away the underlying layer for tiny shapes such as the buckles.

Cut out the stocking front from green, using the stocking pattern. Cut out the stocking back from red, adding ½ inch all around. Also from red, cut a 1- by 7-inch piece for the binding.

Appliqué: Beginning with the larger, underlying shapes, arrange the pieces on the stocking front and fuse them in place. Add top detail shapes. Using a narrow zigzag stitch and matching threads, sew around all pieces. Sew on the beads for eyes and use black thread to straight-stitch whiskers. Glue the pompom noses in place.

Assembly: Fold the binding over the top edge of the stocking front. Zigzag-stitch in place; trim the ends. Center the stocking front on the stocking back, with ½ inch of the back extending on all sides. Topstitch in place, leaving the top edge open. Cut the red felt in a sawtooth pattern, making cuts ⅝ inch wide and ⅜ inch deep (Figure 2). Make two 3½-inch-long tassels from the rug yarn, leaving 12-inch tie ends at the top. Holding the tie ends together, securely tack the last 2 inches of the ties inside the top of the stocking at the back seam. Fold the remaining tie strands in half and knot them together just above the tassel tops, forming a hanging loop above the knot.

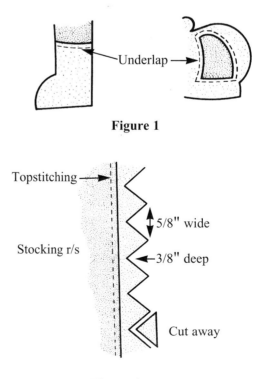

Figure 1

Figure 2

1 square = 1 inch

Nutcracker Stocking Pattern

Santa Claus Stocking

Children love both personalized items and stockings hung by the chimney with care—so a Santa Claus Stocking handmade just for them is sure to please.

Size
Stocking is 16½" tall.

Materials
✦ 20" square of 14-count Aida fabric: blue
✦ 1 yd. of moiré fabric: blue
✦ 1 skein each of 6-strand embroidery floss
(see key for colors)
✦ Assorted trims, ¼" wide
✦ Contrasting and matching threads
✦ Embroidery hoop and tapestry needle
✦ 4 small appliqué stars: gold
✦ Squeezable bottle of fabric paint: pearl
✦ Dressmaker's pencil
✦ Crafts glue

Directions
Note: Before you begin your project, please read "How to Cross-stitch," page 187; "Embroidery Stitches," page 188; and "Enlarging Patterns," page 185. For all seams, place the fabric pieces with right sides together and make ½-inch seams (unless otherwise indicated).

Cross-stitching: With contrasting basting thread, mark the horizontal and vertical centers of the fabric. Center the cross-stitch design on the Aida fabric, matching the fabric center with the arrows on the chart. Following the chart and key, embroider the design. Work cross-stitches with 2 strands of floss; work backstitches with 2 strands of floss. After the embroidery is finished, carefully remove the basting stitches and gently hand-wash the fabric in cold water. Dry it flat and press it on the wrong side.

Cutting: Enlarge the stocking pattern and position it over the embroidered area, checking that the design is centered between the seam allowances and that the top of the design is at the indicated line on the pattern. Use the dressmaker's pencil to draw around the stocking pattern. Cut out the stocking. Cut 3 stocking shapes from the moiré fabric, reversing 2 of them (one reverse shape is for the stocking back and the remaining pair is for the lining).

Assembling: Glue 8-inch lengths of trims at the top seam line, at the top of the embroidery, and above the toe where indicated by the broken line on the chart. Sew the stocking front to the moiré back around the edges, leaving the top edge open. Repeat for the stocking lining. Trim the seams and clip the curves. Turn the stocking right side out and press. With wrong sides together, slip the lining inside the stocking. Turn in ½ inch around the top edge of the stocking and lining; slipstitch the edges together. Fold an 8-inch length of trim in half and tack it securely to the back seam of the stocking for a hanging loop. Personalize the stocking with a desired name, squeezing the fabric paint directly from the bottle to write freehand across the top (or embroider the name, if you prefer). Glue on the stars, scattered near the moon.

Center

Santa Claus Stocking Cross-stitch Chart (top left section)

KEY

Anchor		DMC	Color		Anchor		DMC	Color
2	•	Blanc	White		308	⊙	782	Topaz Dark
387	C	Ecru	Ecru		307	＼	783	Topaz Medium
926	⊐	712	Cream		890	A	729	Old Gold Medium
387	＼	739	Tan Ultra Very Light		305	⋏	725	Topaz
403	■	310	Black		302	O	743	Yellow Medium
850	=	926	Gray Green Medium		300	＼	745	Yellow Light Pale
274			928	Gray Green Very Light		326	●	720	Orange Spice Dark
359	◪	801	Coffee Brown Dark		323	•.	722	Orange Spice Light
379	▽	840	Beige Brown Medium		43	▼	815	Garnet Medium
378	╁	841	Beige Brown Light		46	▪	666	Christmas Red Bright
310	∠	434	Brown Light		9046	✕	321	Christmas Red
1045	⊥	436	Tan		11	Y	350	Coral Medium
388	T	842	Beige Brown Very Light					

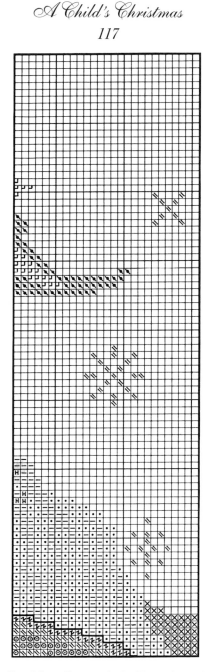

Santa Claus Stocking Cross-stitch Chart (top right section)

Anchor		DMC	Color
9	↵	352	Coral Light
6	F	353	Peach Flesh
895	□	223	Shell Pink Light
35	S	3705	Melon Dark
31	Y	3708	Melon Light
1011	Γ	948	Peach Flesh Very Light
100	✳	327	Violet Very Dark
99	P	552	Violet Medium
98	L	553	Violet
96	⅃	554	Violet Light
928	人	3761	Sky Blue Very Light
869	⌐	3743	Antique Violet Very Light
148	◥	311	Navy Blue Medium
979	I	312	Navy Blue Light
978	V	322	Navy Blue Very Light
169	Z	806	Peacock Blue Dark

Anchor		DMC	Color
1033	H	932	Antique Blue Light
1039	J	518	Wedgewood Light
1038	+	519	Sky Blue
1031	—	3753	Antique Blue Ultra Very Light
218	▲	890	Pistachio Ultra Dark
212	<	561	Jade Very Dark
210	/	562	Jade Medium
262	(	3363	Pine Green Medium
858	I	524	Fern Green Very Light

BACKSTITCH (Use 2 strands)

403	⌐	310	Black

FRENCH KNOT (Use 2 strands, 1 wrap)

2	⊕	Blanc	White, Santa's eyes

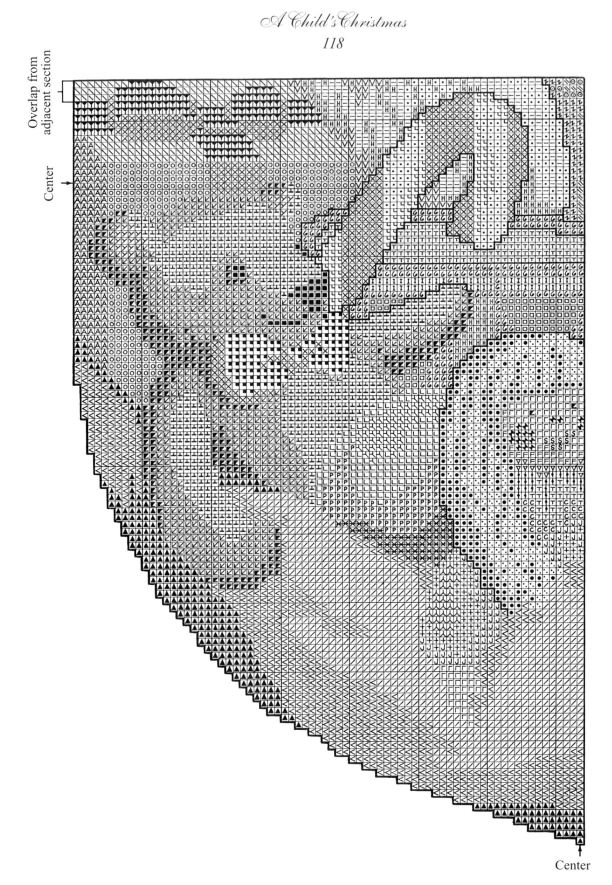

Santa Claus Stocking Cross-stitch Chart (lower left section)

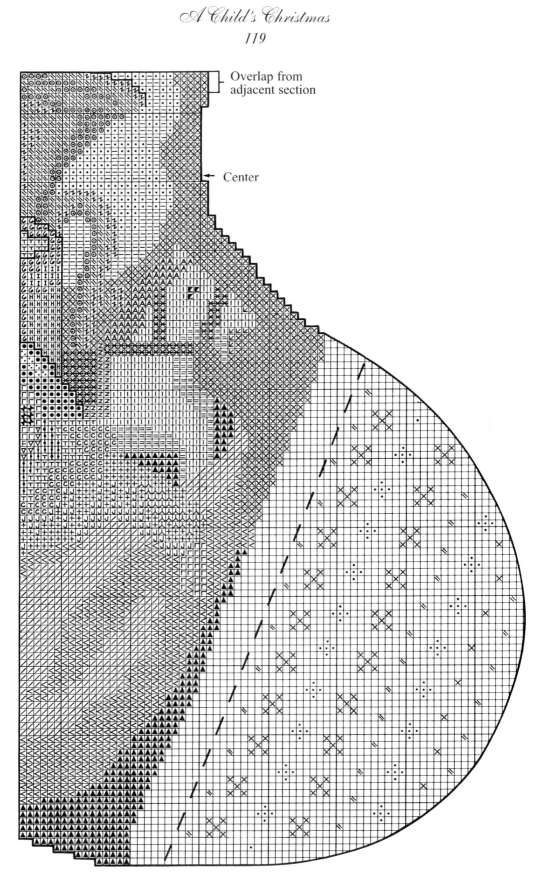

Overlap from adjacent section

Center

Santa Claus Stocking Cross-stitch Chart (lower right section)

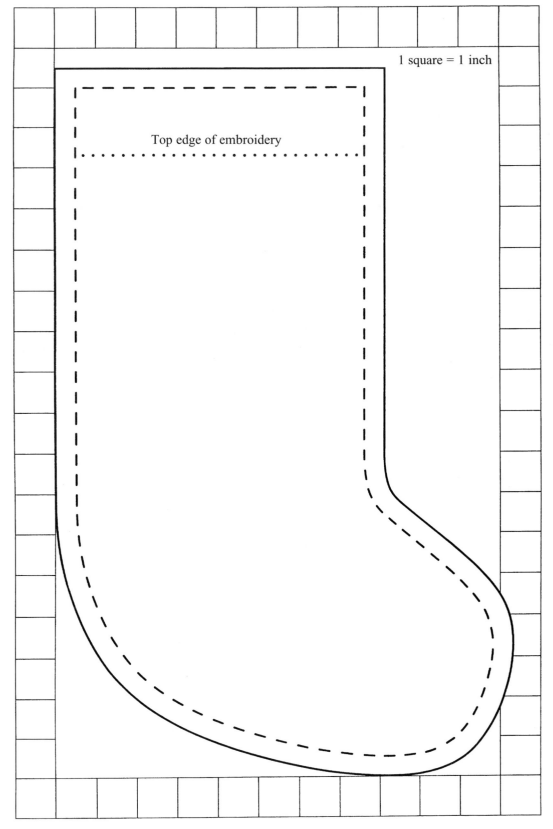

1 square = 1 inch

Top edge of embroidery

Santa Claus Stocking Pattern

A Sacred Season

Silent night, Holy night,
All is calm, all is bright.
'Round yon Virgin
Mother and Child,
Holy Infant
so tender and mild.

It is a custom in Christian homes
all over the world to display the nativity
scene of Mary, Joseph, and the infant
Jesus surrounded by angels, shepherds,
and kings bearing gifts. The projects
in this chapter provide beautiful
examples of that tradition that will be
cherished for many years.

Nativity Paper Cuttings

*In the Nativity Paper Cutting on the left,
openings backed with colorful tissue papers
suggest the splendor of stained glass.
The same simple pattern appears on the right in
subtle blue and white paper and has a more
ethereal quality.*

Size
Mounted paper cuttings are 11" × 14".

Materials

For Either Version:
 ◆ Picture frame with 11" × 14" opening: gold
 ◆ 11" × 14" self-sticking mounting board
 ◆ Tracing and transfer papers
 ◆ Sheet of plain paper
 ◆ Crafts knife with extra blades
 ◆ Spray adhesive

For Blue and White Version:
 ◆ 8" × 10" sheet of stiff paper: white
 ◆ 11" × 14" sheet of stiff paper: cobalt blue
 ◆ 11" × 14" double mat with 8" × 10" opening: gold over black

For Stained Glass Paper Version:
 ◆ 8" × 10" sheet of stiff paper: black
 ◆ 11" × 14" sheet of stiff paper: pale yellow
 ◆ 11" × 14" double mat with 8" × 10" opening: white over black
 ◆ Tissue paper: turquoise (A), royal blue (B), light purple (C), light green (D), Kelly green (E), magenta (F), yellow (G), medium purple (H), and dark purple (I)

Directions

Either Version: Fold the white or the black paper in half lengthwise. Transfer the half-design cutting pattern onto the paper along the fold line (see "Transferring Patterns," page 186). Using the crafts knife, cut out the shaded shapes through both layers at once with crisp, clean cuts. Change the blades as necessary. Open up the paper and press it flat. Spray the back of the cut paper with the adhesive.

Blue and White Version: Cover the self-sticking mounting board with the cobalt blue paper, smoothing out any wrinkles with the palm of your hand. Trim the edges if necessary. Place the gold/black double mat over the mounting board and outline the opening lightly with a pencil. Remove the double mat. Center the white paper cutting within the outline of the opening and press it in place. To protect the paper cutting, place a plain sheet of paper over it before you use the side of your palm to smooth out any wrinkles and eliminate any air pockets; then remove the plain sheet of paper. Reposition the mat on the mounted paper cutting and place them in the frame.

Stained Glass Paper Cutting: Following the placement diagram for colors and the cutting pattern for size, cut the tissue paper to fit the areas marked, adding a ¼-inch overlap all around. Position the tissue paper pieces on the wrong side of the black paper cutting and gently rub them in place to secure them. The cradle shapes will be covered with both yellow and magenta tissue paper; place the yellow next to the cutting. Spray the back of the finished stained glass paper cutting with adhesive.

Cover the self-sticking mounting board with pale yellow paper, smoothing out the wrinkles with the palm of your hand. Trim the edges if necessary. Place the white/black double mat over the mounting board and outline the opening lightly with a pencil. Remove the double mat. Center the stained glass paper cutting within the opening outline, and press it in place. To protect the paper cutting, place a plain sheet of paper over it before you use the side of your palm to smooth out any wrinkles and eliminate any air pockets; then remove the plain sheet of paper. Reposition the mat on the mounted paper cutting and place them in the frame.

Nativity Paper Cuttings
Cutting Pattern
(actual size)

Fold line

Three Wise Men

The three elegantly robed kings carrying gifts of gold, frankincense, and myrrh proceed on their journey in this striking vignette for a tabletop or mantel. These simple shapes covered with rich fabrics evoke the majesty of Christmas.

Size
Wise men are 12" tall.

Materials
- Foamcore™ board, ⅛" to ³⁄₁₆" thick: gold
- ¼ yd. of brocade fabric: patterned with metallic gold threads
- ¼ yd. of silk fabric: peacock blue
- ¼ yd. of panne velvet fabric: royal blue
- Assorted ribbons, trims, and rickrack: gold
- Polyester stuffing
- Three 4½" × 6½" wood bases
- Spray paint: gold
- Assorted small sequins and jewels
- Tracing paper
- Crafts knife
- Spray adhesive
- Hot-glue gun and glue sticks

Directions
Foundations: Spray-paint the wrong side of the Foamcore board with 2 coats of gold. Allow to dry. Enlarge the wise men designs and trace onto tracing paper to use as patterns (see "Enlarging Patterns" and "Transferring Patterns," pages 185 and 186; note that the order of wise men in the pattern on page 128 is different from that in the photograph). Make 2 patterns for each wise man. Spray the back of 1 pattern of each wise man with adhesive and position it on the Foamcore. Using the crafts knife and making crisp, clean cuts, cut

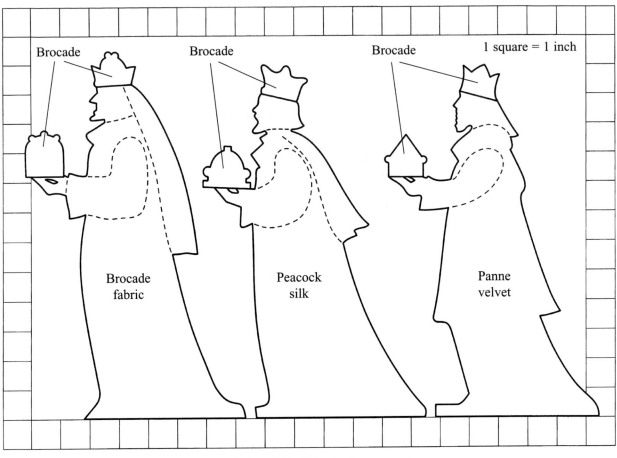

Three Wise Men Patterns

out the wise men shapes. Carefully peel off the pattern. Using the broken line on the patterns as a guide, pencil the arm outline on each wise man.

Clothes: Using the second paper pattern and the appropriate fabric, cut out clothes for the front of each wise man, adding a ½-inch seam allowance all around. Reverse the paper pattern and cut out clothes for the backs without adding any seam allowance. Cover both sides of each wise man with the polyester stuffing and glue in place. Define the arms by leaving an unstuffed space around each arm shape. Outline each arm with a line of glue so that the fabric will be glued directly onto the

Foamcore. Position the fabric front, pulling the seam allowance over the edges to the back. Clip the corners and curves and glue in place. Position the fabric back, covering the raw edges of the front piece, and glue in place.

Trims: Cut out the crowns and gift shapes from the brocade fabric and glue in place. Reverse the patterns and cut out the crowns and gifts for the backs and glue in place. Glue flat trim around the edges of each Foamcore at the hand, head, and crown. Following the photograph, glue on the trims, rickrack, jewels, and sequins as desired. Spray-paint each wood base gold. Allow to dry. Glue a wise man in the center of each base.

Nativity Sampler

*This exquisite design depicts
the birth of Jesus with a multitude of intricate
stitches and radiant color. It is sure to become a
family heirloom to be treasured
for generations.*

Size

Embroidered area of sampler is 17½" × 13".

Materials

- 19" × 15" piece of 14-count Aida™ fabric: royal blue
- 1 skein each of 6-strand embroidery floss (see key for colors)
- 1 skein each of rayon embroidery floss (see key for colors)
- 1 skein each of metallic embroidery floss: gold and silver
- Flat trim, ⅛" wide: gold
- Contrasting thread
- Beads: silver and gold
- Sewing thread
- Embroidery hoop and needle
- Frame (optional; see Note, page 131)

Directions

Basic Cross-stitching: See "How to Cross-stitch" and "Embroidery Stitches," pages 187 and 188. With contrasting basting thread, mark the horizontal and vertical centers of the fabric. Center the cross-stitch design on the Aida fabric, matching the fabric center with the arrows on the chart. See the following for which detail areas are to be worked with special stitches. Following the chart and key, work the cross-stitch areas with 3 strands of floss. Where there is a half symbol or two partial symbols in one square, work a partial stitch matching color(s) to surrounding stitches. These partial stitches are used along edges of shapes to give better contours.

Detail Areas: See key for colors on special stitches. *Border pattern:* Using 2 strands, work straight stitches diagonally across 1 square of fabric (Figure 1).

Outlines: Use 1 strand to work the backstitches.

Shepherd's vest (two-color cross-stitch): Using 3 strands of lighter color, work the underlying diagonal of each cross-stitch (note

Border pattern

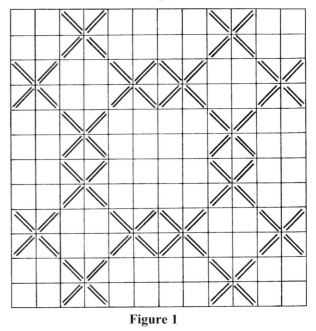

Figure 1

that the direction of the underlying stitches changes [Figure 2a] to balance the direction of the top diagonals [Figure 2b], which are indicated on the chart). Work the top diagonals with 3 strands of the darker color. If you prefer, use traditional rice stitch for the vest.

Shepherd's waistband and headband (couching stitch, indicated on chart): Use four 6-strand pieces of floss and couch with one 6-strand piece.

Shepherd's vest

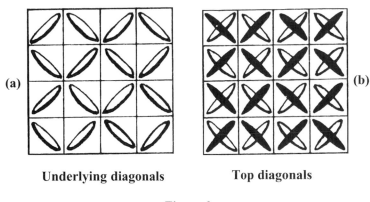

(a)   (b)

Underlying diagonals   **Top diagonals**

Figure 2

Faces: To work eyes (indicated by circle on chart), work small satin stitches at circle, using 2 strands of Blue Medium for Mary, the baby, and the angel, and 2 strands of Topaz Ultra Very Dark for all others. With 1 strand of Black, make a tiny French knot in the center of each eye, wrapping around the needle once. See key for other facial details.

Angel's headband: Use 2 strands to work lazy-daisy stitches, indicated by a broken line on the chart. Work stitches scattered along each side of the line.

Lamb and sheep: Use 4 strands to work French knots, wrapping around the needle twice. Fill in the blank areas of the bodies with closely spaced French knots.

Kings' tassels: Work a tassel over squares just to the right of each T mark, working white tassels on hatband and shoulder of left king and Topaz Light tassels on front collar edge on middle king. For each tassel, cut two 6-strand pieces of floss, each 1 inch long. Holding the floss pieces together, fold them in half, and tack them in place 1 square below the top fold, covering the desired square. (The tacking stitches form the tassels' ties.)

Finishing: After all the cross-stitching and the embroidery are finished, carefully remove the basting stitches and gently hand-wash the fabric in cold water. Dry it flat and press it on the wrong side. Sew the beads to the angel's headband, the kings' treasure boxes, and the king's cuff (on king at far left). Position the flat trim in an oval separating the design area and the border, omitting the trim where the design area extends past the oval (at the sheep, a king's robe, and the angel's wings). Tack the trim in place.

Note: If you would like an heirloom-quality cross-stitch project, we recommend taking the completed, pressed piece to a professional framer who has had experience framing needlework. You've already invested your time; it's worth protecting that investment!

KEY

Anchor		DMC	Color
2	•	Blanc	White
403	◆	310	Black
295	ʎ	726	Topaz Light
288	Y	445	Lemon Light
333	A	900	Burnt Orange Dark
329	O	3340	Apricot Medium
74	V	3354	Dusty Rose Light
868	P	3779	Terra Cotta Ultra Very Light
102	▼	550	Violet Very Dark
1019	M	315	Antique Mauve Very Dark
110	+	208	Lavender Very Dark
342	J	211	Lavender Light
161	▀	826	Blue Medium
167	T	3766	Peacock Blue Light
140	⌿	3755	Baby Blue
158	⫯	747	Sky Blue Ultra Very Light
683	▲	500	Blue Green Very Dark
218	⦣	319	Pistachio Very Dark
214	L	368	Pistachio Light
381	◥	938	Coffee Brown Ultra Dark
359	⑊	801	Coffee Brown Dark
310	Y	780	Topaz Ultra Very Dark
307	◤	783	Topaz Medium
374	⧗	420	Hazel Nut Brown Dark
361	=	738	Tan Very Light
881	┌	945	Sportsman Flesh Medium
1010	|	951	Sportsman Flesh Very Light
275	┘	746	Off-white
1041	■	844	Beaver Gray Ultra Dark
399	Z	318	Steel Gray Light

DMC #10 Metallic

	C	280	Gold
	S	281	Silver

Marlitt Rayon Floss

	—	800	White
	▽	820	Lemon
	⋌	831	Dark Coral
	⋇	894	Dark Red
	ɕ	893	Red
	<	1213	Light Pink
	◣	859	Dark Purple
	┘	858	Medium Purple
	╲	857	Light Purple
	⁄	1214	Light Lavender
	◢	836	Dark Blue
	X	835	Medium Blue
	╱	1059	Light Blue
	┴	1066	Dark Seafoam
	└	832	Light Seafoam
	●	1067	Green
	I	845	Gray

Anchor		DMC	Color
BLENDED-COLOR CROSS-STITCH (Use 3 strands)			
398	⁘	415	Pearl Gray (2), used together with
234		762	Pearl Gray Very Light (1)
TWO-COLOR CROSS-STITCH (Use 3 strands)			
5975	☒	356	Terra Cotta Medium, top diagonals on vest
882		758	Terra Cotta Very Light, underlying diagonals
COUCHING STITCH			
1014	⧣	355	Terra Cotta Dark,
882		758	Terra Cotta Very Light
FRENCH KNOT (Use 4 strands/2 wraps)			
1040	⊘	647	Beaver Gray Medium, sheep
397	⊙	3024	Brown Gray Very Light, sheep
391		3033	Mocha Brown Very Light, fill in blank area on sheep
SATIN STITCH (Use 2 strands)			
5975		356	Terra Cotta Medium, mouths
STRAIGHT STITCH			
398	—	415	Pearl Gray (2), used with
234		762	Pearl Gray Very Light (1), middle King's eyebrows
359	—	801	Coffee Brown Dark (2), Mary's eyebrows
359	—	801	Coffee Brown Dark (3), eyebrows for all but Mary and middle King
BACKSTITCH (Use 1 strand)			
382	⌙	3371	Black Brown

DMC #10 Metallic

BORDER STITCH (Use 2 strands)			
		280	Gold

Marlitt Rayon Floss

BACKSTITCH (Use 2 strands)			
	⌙	836	Dark Blue, banner letters
LAZY-DAISY STITCH (Use 2 strands)			
	– –	1066	Dark Seafoam, angel's head band

Nativity Sampler Cross-stitch Chart (top left section)

top left	top center	top right
lower left	lower center	lower right

Overlap from adjacent section   Center

Nativity Sampler Cross-stitch Chart (top center section)

top left	top center	top right
lower left	lower center	lower right

Nativity Sampler Cross-stitch Chart (top right section)

Center

Overlap from adjacent section

Nativity Sampler Cross-stitch Chart (lower left section)

top left	top center	top right
lower left	lower center	lower right

Center

Nativity Sampler Cross-stitch Chart (lower center section)

Overlap from adjacent section

Nativity Sampler Cross-stitch Chart (lower right section)

top left	top center	top right
lower left	lower center	lower right

Nature's Bounty

On the first day of Christmas,
My true love sent to me
A partridge in a pear tree.

Celebrate Christmas with a collection
of decorative accents inspired by nature's gifts to
us the year around. The rich colors and
textures of the Decoupage Fruit Plates help
create eye-catching decorations for the home,
and Fruitful Gift Wraps beautifully
symbolize nature's bountiful harvests. Queen
Anne's Lace Snowflake Ornaments, Dough
Ornaments, the Strawberry Jewel Ornament,
and Fruit and Ribbon Ornaments all create a
colorful cornucopia on the tree.

Decoupage Fruit Plates

These Decoupage Fruit Plates revive the popular Victorian craft of decoupage. Cutouts of lush fruits are applied to clear glass plates, backed with antique map tissue paper, and sprayed gold. Make color photocopies of your favorite fruit prints and create a set of these luxurious-looking plates. To preserve them, use your fruit plates for decoration only.

Size
Plates are 9" or the size you select.

Materials
✦ 4 clear glass plates with flat bottoms
✦ Reproductions or color photocopies of fruit botanicals
✦ Tissue paper with "Old World Map" or desired pattern
✦ Spray paint: gold
✦ Foam paintbrush, 1" wide
✦ Acrylic gel medium
✦ Sharp, pointed scissors
✦ Medium writer pen: gold
✦ Paper for pattern

Directions
Note: Allow gel and paint to dry thoroughly between steps. Before beginning, wash and dry the plates.

Fruit Decoupage: Carefully cut out the fruit botanicals. Using the foam paintbrush, paint the front side of the fruit motif with acrylic gel medium. Place the motif on the back of the plate. Press with your finger to secure it to the plate and to remove any air bubbles. Clip and overlap the paper as needed so that it adheres to the rim of the plate. On the back of the plate, use the writer pen to outline the fruit motif as desired; outline the rim of the plate.

Tissue: To make a pattern, lay the plate upside down on the paper, trace the plate outline, and cut it out, adding ½ inch all around. Use the pattern to rough-cut a circle from the tissue paper. Cut slits from the edge of the tissue paper inward to the center flat area of the plate, spacing the slits about every 1½ inches.

Cover the back of the plate with a thin coat of acrylic gel medium. Center the front side of the tissue paper on the back of the plate. Overlap the tissue at the slits to adhere the paper to the plate, making additional clips as needed to keep the tissue flat against the plate. Trim any excess tissue around the edge. Rub with your finger to secure and to remove any air bubbles; then burnish with your finger. Wipe any excess gel medium from the front of the plate with a damp paper towel. Allow to dry for 1 hour.

Finish: Paint the back of the plate with a second coat of gel medium. Repeat for all 4 plates. Spray the back of each plate with 2 coats of gold paint, allowing the paint to dry between coats. Clean the plates by wiping gently with a damp cloth, but do not wash them.

Fruit and Ribbon Ornaments

Brightly hued artificial fruits tied with ombré wire-edged ribbons become stunning Christmas balls. Fruit and Ribbon Ornaments are lightweight, so they're perfect for hanging from the tree. Or cluster them in a favorite bowl and display them on a tabletop.

Size
Ornaments are about 3" or size desired.

Materials
- ✦ Assorted artificial fruits
- ✦ Dried pomegranates (heavier than artificial fruits)
- ✦ About ½ yd. of assorted flat trims, cords, and braids for each ornament: gold
- ✦ 12" length of wire-edged ombré ribbon for each ornament: assorted colors
- ✦ 8" length of thin cord for each ornament: gold
- ✦ Upholstery tacks
- ✦ Hot-glue gun and glue sticks

Directions
Following the photograph, arrange a length of trim around the bottom of the fruit and up the sides to the top; glue in place. Arrange and glue a second trim, crossing the first on the bottom, in the same manner. If desired, add narrow cord in same manner, spacing it evenly between the previous trims. Press an upholstery tack into the bottom of the fruit where the trims intersect.

Cut 12-inch lengths of ribbon and tie into bows. Glue one to the top of each fruit. Trim the ends as desired and drape them gracefully. For each ornament, fold an 8-inch length of thin cord in half and knot the ends. Glue it to the top of the bow for a hanging loop.

A Trio of Topiaries

*Three tabletop trees fashioned from
natural and scrap-basket materials are center-
pieces with style. Tiny red balls and festive
tapestry ribbon make the Pinecone Topiary (left)
a contemporary version of an old favorite. Fabric
strips lend a soft charm to the Rag Topiary
(center); ribbons would also be attractive.
Dried, brightly colored blossoms adorn
the Zinnia Topiary (right).*

Pinecone Topiary

Size
Topiary is 22" tall.

Materials
- Plastic foam cone, 15" tall
- 10" length of dowel, ½" diameter
- Terra-cotta flowerpot, 5" tall
- Small pinecones, sweet gum balls, nuts, and pods
- Cinnamon sticks
- Reindeer moss
- Decorative berries and small glass balls: red
- ¾ yd. of wire-edged tapestry-patterned ribbon, 2⅝" wide
- 3 sheets of copper leaf and gold-leaf adhesive (or use copper metallic paint)
- Linoleum paste: brown
- Floral clay
- Stones to weight container
- Hot-glue gun and glue sticks
- Spray sealer

Directions
Topiary: Cover the work surface with newspaper and plastic wrap. Keep cone on covered work surface and turn it instead of picking it up. Starting at lower edge of the cone, cover 2 inches with a thick coat of the linoleum paste. Arrange and attach the pinecones, sweet gum balls, nuts, and pods, pressing them firmly into the paste until they are secure. Working a 2-inch section at a time, cover the cone halfway up. Allow it to dry. Continue to cover the top half of the cone when the bottom half is dry and secure. This will keep the upper pinecones from pushing the lower ones off the cone form. When the cone is dry, arrange and hot-glue the balls and berries in place.

Pot: Cover the sides, rim, and lip of the flowerpot with the gold-leaf adhesive. Apply the copper leaf, smoothing it in place with your finger. Patch areas with small pieces of leaf until the pot is completely covered. Spray it with sealer and allow it to dry.

Assembly: If possible, have someone help you with the next step. Insert the dowel into the center of the bottom of the cone until it is about 2 inches deep; glue it in place. Glue the bottom edge of the dowel to the bottom of the pot, adding some floral clay for extra support. Keeping the topiary upright, fill the pot with stones all around the dowel. Cover the top of the stones with floral clay. Glue the dowel to the surrounding clay. Cover the top of the clay base with reindeer moss. Glue cinnamon sticks around the dowel. Allow to dry. Tie the ribbon into a bow around the stem. Trim the ends. Shape the ribbon bow and drape the ends gracefully.

Rag Topiary

Size
Topiary is 22" tall.

Materials
- Plastic foam cone, 15" tall
- 10" length of dowel, ½" diameter
- Terra-cotta flowerpot, 5" tall
- Fabric strips or ribbon, ⅜" to 1" wide
- 2 yd. of ribbon, 1¼" wide: red
- Spray fabric stiffener
- 3 sheets of silver leaf and gold-leaf adhesive (or use silver metallic paint)
- Sheet moss
- Floral wire, 20 gauge
- Wire cutters
- Floral clay
- Stones to weight container
- Hot-glue gun and glue sticks
- Spray sealer

Directions
Topiary: Cut the wire into 2-inch lengths. Cut the ribbon or fabric strips into 12-inch lengths.

Make each strip into a bow by folding one end over the other (Figure 1) and then twisting a 2-inch length of wire around the center. Spray the bow with fabric stiffener and attach it to the cone by inserting the wire ends into the foam. Cover the sides of the cone completely with bows.

Pot: Cover the sides, rim, and lip of the flowerpot with gold-leaf adhesive. Apply the silver leaf, smoothing it in place with your finger. Patch areas with small pieces of leaf until the pot is completely covered. Spray it with sealer and allow it to dry.

Assembly: If possible, have someone help you with the next step. Insert the dowel into the center of the bottom of the cone until it is about 2 inches deep; glue it in place. Glue the bottom edge of the dowel to the bottom of the pot, adding some floral clay for extra support. Keeping the topiary upright, fill the pot with stones all around the dowel. Cover the top of the stones with floral clay. Glue the dowel to the surrounding clay. Cover the top of the clay base with sheet moss; glue in place. Twist 1 yard of red ribbon around the dowel to cover it, gluing ends in place. Wrap the remaining red ribbon around the pot and tie it into a bow. Trim the ends and drape them gracefully.

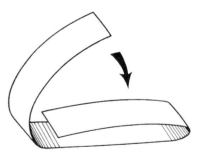

Figure 1

Zinnia Topiary

Size
Topiary is 22" tall.

Materials
✦ Plastic foam cone, 15" tall
✦ 10" length of dowel, ½" diameter
✦ Terra-cotta flowerpot, 5" tall
✦ Dried zinnia blooms (about 14 red flowers)
✦ Green reindeer moss
✦ Small amount of sheet moss
✦ ¾ yd. of wire-edged ribbon: red
✦ 2 yd. of cord, ⅛" diameter: gold
✦ 3 sheets of gold leaf and gold-leaf adhesive (or use gold metallic paint)
✦ Floral clay
✦ Stones to weight container
✦ Hot-glue gun and glue sticks
✦ Spray sealer

Directions
Topiary: Cover the cone with reindeer moss; glue it in place. Following the photograph, arrange zinnia blooms on the cone. Glue the blooms, pressing them firmly until secure.

Pot: Cover the sides, rim, and lip of the flowerpot with the gold-leaf adhesive. Apply the gold leaf, smoothing it in place with your finger. Patch areas with small pieces of leaf until the pot is completely covered. Spray it with sealer and allow it to dry.

Assembly: Follow assembly directions for the Rag Topiary (earlier) until sheet moss has been glued in place. Then wrap the stem with gold cord, securing the ends with glue. Tie the ribbon into a bow around the stem. Shape the ribbon bow. Trim and drape ends gracefully.

Musical Trees

*Musical wrapping paper—or actual antique
sheet music—affixed to graceful tree shapes gives
these clever decorations a note of whimsy.
Interlocking pieces make them easy to store when
they're finished performing for the holidays.*

Sizes

Trees are 7" and 9" tall.

Materials

✦ 1 sheet of Foamcore, ³⁄₁₆" thick
✦ 2 sheets of Latin or Christmas music
✦ 3 yd. of ribbon, ³⁄₁₆" wide: red with gold stripes
✦ Tracing and transfer papers
✦ Crafts knife
✦ Spray adhesive
✦ Hot-glue gun and glue sticks
✦ Spray sealer

Directions

Spray the wrong side of the music paper with adhesive. Attach the paper to both sides of the Foamcore board, smoothing out wrinkles with the palm of your hand. Enlarge the tree patterns and transfer them to the Foamcore, making both trees for each size (see "Enlarging Patterns" and "Transferring Patterns," pages 185 and 186). Cut out the tree shapes, using the crafts knife to make clean cuts. Cut out the slot in each tree. Glue the ribbon around the outer edges, except along the bottom of the tree. Spray with 2 coats of sealer. Slip the same-sized tree pieces together, interlocking the slots at right angles.

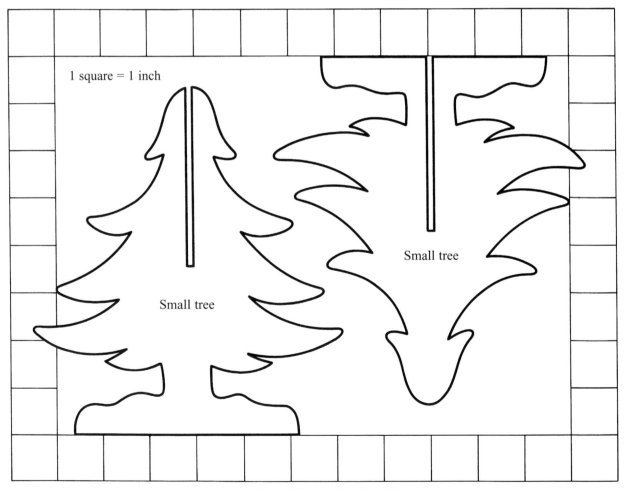

1 square = 1 inch

Small tree

Small tree

Musical Trees Pattern for Small Tree

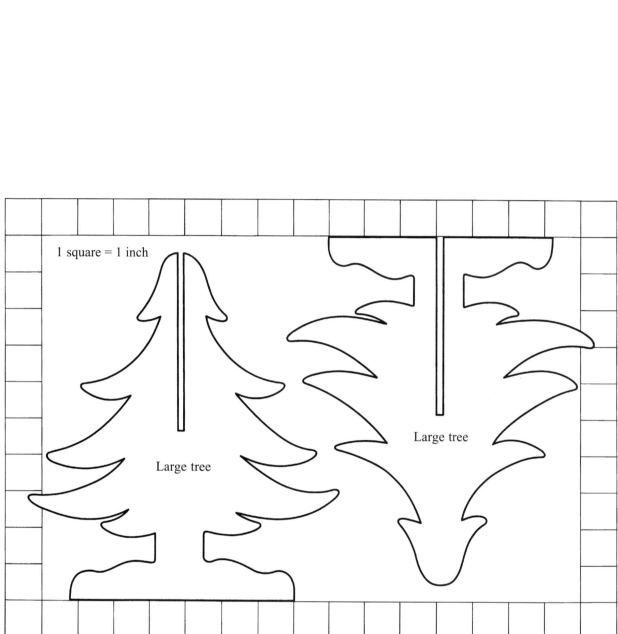

1 square = 1 inch

Large tree

Large tree

Musical Trees Pattern for Large Tree

Flower-Stamped Wraps, Ribbons, and Cards

These richly colored and embellished gift accessories add a handmade, personal touch to presents for everyone on your list. Artists of all skill levels can help stamp wrapping paper, ribbons, and cards with as much detail as desired.

Size
Wrappings and cards are sizes desired.

Materials
✦ Assorted floral and Christmas-motif rubber stamps
✦ Stamp pads: gold, silver, or desired colors
✦ Wire-edged taffeta ribbon, 1" to 2" wide: assorted jewel tones with gold edge
✦ Shiny wrapping paper: gold foil and assorted jewel tones
✦ Blank note cards and envelopes

Directions
On a flat surface, lay out the wrapping paper and the ribbons.

Press the stamp onto the ink pad, covering the entire surface of the rubber stamp evenly with ink. Center the stamp on the ribbon and press it to print the motif clearly. Continue to stamp at regular intervals or as desired along the lengths of the ribbons and on the wrapping papers. Clean the stamps with a paper towel as necessary to keep the motifs clear and crisp. Position and stamp the motifs on the front of the note cards, using different stamps and colors as desired. Allow to dry.

Wrap gifts with the wrapping paper and tie the ribbons around the packages. Tie the ends into bows and trim the ends as desired.

Dough Ornaments

Made of simple ingredients, Dough Ornaments are a favorite with crafters of all ages and can be as detailed and realistic as you like. Play some festive music and enjoy a family activity while they slow-bake in the oven.

Sizes
Ornaments are 2" to 3" across.

Materials
✦ Dough for ornaments (see page 155)
✦ Glycerin
✦ Instant coffee or food coloring (optional)
✦ Cloves, mustard seeds, and whole peppercorns
✦ Cookie cutters: round, diamond, and scalloped-edge shapes
✦ Knife and metal spatula
✦ Mixing bowl and electric mixer
✦ Wooden spoon
✦ Rolling pin
✦ Noncoated cookie sheets
✦ Comb
✦ Tweezers
✦ Plastic straw
✦ Toothpicks
✦ Polyurethane sealer
✦ Foam paintbrush, 1" wide
✦ Brass wire and wire cutters for hanging loops
✦ 8" length of raffia for each ornament
✦ Hot-glue gun and glue sticks
✦ Garlic press (optional)
✦ Textured buttons (optional)

Figure 1

Directions

Dough Shapes: Using a mixer, combine 2 cups of all-purpose flour with 1 cup of salt and ½ cup of water. Add instant coffee combined with water to a small amount of dough to make the second color or use food coloring as desired. Add more water a little at a time and a few drops of glycerin until the dough is a workable texture. Adding too much water will make the dough rise and will cause it to crack when it dries. Store the dough in an airtight container until you are ready to work. Roll the dough to a ¼-inch thickness directly onto the cookie sheets. Using cookie cutters, cut shapes as desired, remove any excess dough around the shapes for clean edges. See Figure 1 for the shapes and placement of details.

To make a basket, cut off the top third of the circle shape. Roll out some dough with the palm of your hand to make two ¼-inch-diameter rolls. Twist them together for the basket handles (Figure 2); shape the curve and secure the ends to the basket (to secure, moisten the pieces with water and press them together). To make a wreath, make 2 rolls and twist them together (Figure 2), shape into a circle, and secure the ends.

Details: Use the straw to cut out a small hole in each solid ornament for hanging (see later for hanging the basket and wreath). Flatten small pieces of dough to make leaf, acorn, and apple shapes. Using the comb or toothpicks, create basket weave textures and leaf details. Decorate the edges of some ornaments by pressing with the comb or by pricking with a toothpick. Using the tweezers to handle tiny pieces, arrange the shapes around the ornaments as desired. Moisten the surfaces and press the pieces together to secure. Roll tiny balls of dough to make grapes and attach several balls together on an ornament to make bunches. Use cloves as stems for the apples. Press peppercorns, mustard seeds, and cloves into the dough as desired.

Finish: Baking the ornaments too quickly will cause the dough to rise. Bake at 150° for 1 hour, then at 200° for ½ hour, then at 250° for ½ hour, and finally at 270° for 1 hour. Allow to cool. Paint both sides of the ornaments with polyurethane. Allow to dry.

To hang the basket and the wreath shapes, cut a 1½-inch length of wire. Bend it in half and glue the ends to the back of the ornament at the top with the loop exposed. Thread an 8-inch length of raffia through the wire loop or through the hole in the ornament for a hanging loop and knot the ends to secure.

Suggestion: To make your own designs, try using these additional techniques: Use textured buttons to stamp designs on the ornaments. Press the dough through a garlic press to make a furlike texture. Check your kitchen drawers for other tools you can use creatively.

Figure 2

Strawberry Jewel Ornament

Someone special will appreciate the time and effort required to make this glittering Strawberry Jewel Ornament. Covered in red sequins and topped with a green velvet cap, this little gem adds a touch of opulence to a fir tree's boughs.

Size
Ornament is about 2" across.

Materials
- 3" cube of floral foam
- 2" square of velvet: green
- 16" length of thin cord: gold
- Sequins: red
- Brass craft pins
- Ornament top: gold
- Tracing paper
- Hot-glue gun and glue sticks

Directions
Shape the floral foam into a strawberry shape by squeezing and compressing it with your fingers. Completely cover the foam with sequins by securing each sequin with a pin. Trace the calyx pattern and pin it to the velvet. Cut the calyx from the velvet and glue it to the top of the strawberry. Glue on the gold ornament top. Cut and thread two 8-inch lengths of cord through the loop on the ornament top. Knot the ends together for a hanging loop.

Calyx Pattern (actual size)

Fruitful Gift Wraps

Jewel-toned wrapping papers, gold-edged organdy ribbons, and colorful artificial fruits create presents almost too pretty to open. The miniature fruits can be saved for future gift giving, displayed in a small fruit bowl, or even kept as embellishments for the Christmas tree.

Sizes
Boxes are sizes desired.

Materials
+ Assorted gift boxes
+ Shiny wrapping paper: gold foil and assorted jewel tones
+ Sheer wire-edged ribbon, 1" wide: assorted jewel tones with gold edges
+ Assorted small artificial fruit picks: grapes, pears, berries, and other fruits as desired
+ Florist's wire and wire cutters or hot-glue gun and glue sticks

Directions
Wrap the packages with paper as desired. Tie ribbons around the packages. Tie the ends into large bows; make double bows on some packages. Trim the ends as desired and drape them gracefully. Using a hot-glue gun or florist's wire, attach the wire fruit picks to the center of the bows.

Floral Cut-Paper Wreath

The wreath has been a part of religious and social celebrations since ancient times. The one shown here in simple and striking form is made by carefully cutting designs in paper.

Size
Mounted cutout is 14" square.

Materials
✦ 10" square of stiff paper: white
✦ 14" square of heavyweight paper: red
✦ 14" square double mat with 10" square opening: green over gold
✦ Picture frame with 14" square opening: gold
✦ 14" square self-stick mounting board
✦ Tracing and transfer papers
✦ Sheet of plain paper
✦ Paper punch
✦ Crafts knife with extra blades
✦ Spray adhesive

Directions
Cutting: See "Enlarging Patterns" and "Transferring Patterns," pages 185 and 186. Fold the white paper in half. Enlarge the half-design cutting pattern and transfer it onto the paper along the fold line. Using the crafts knife, cut out the floral ring and the shaded shapes through both layers at once with crisp,

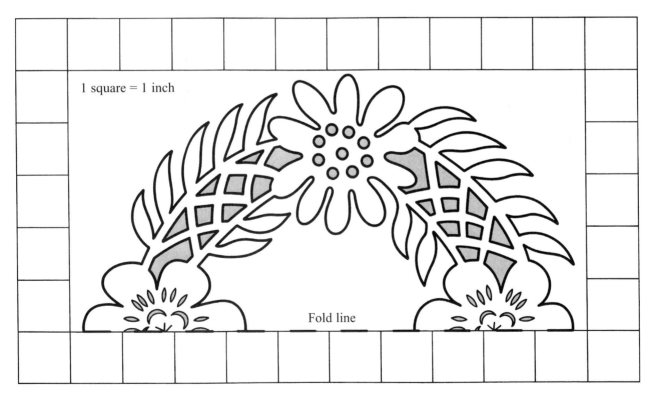

1 square = 1 inch

Fold line

Floral Cut-Paper Wreath Cutting Pattern

clean cuts. Do not cut the flower centers while the paper is folded. Change the blades as needed. Open up the paper and press it flat. Cut out the slits and curved shapes in two of the flower centers as indicated, leaving small bridges of paper so that the center is not cut out completely. Use the paper punch to make the holes in the centers of the other two flowers.

Assembly: Spray the back of the cutout with adhesive. Cover the self-sticking mounting board with the red paper, smoothing out any wrinkles with the palm of your hand. Trim the edges if necessary. Place the double mat over the mounting board and outline the opening lightly with a pencil. Remove the double mat. Center the white cutout within the outline of the opening and press it in place. To protect the cutout, place a plain sheet of paper over it before you use the side of your palm to smooth out any wrinkles and eliminate any air pockets; then remove the plain sheet of paper. Reposition the mat on the mounted cutout and place them in the frame.

Golden Shell Ornaments

Gilded and embellished with sprigs of greenery, the souvenirs of a summer beach make easy, festive Christmas ornaments, just right for stuffing stockings or welcoming guests during the holidays.

Size
Ornaments are about 2½" or the size of the shell you select.

Materials
✦ Assorted medium-sized seashells
✦ Acrylic paint: gold
✦ Small paintbrushes
✦ 8" length of satin ribbon for each ornament, ¼" wide: assorted colors
✦ Sprigs of artificial greens
✦ Red berries
✦ Hot-glue gun and glue sticks

Directions
Paint the shells gold and allow them to dry. Following the photograph, glue greens and berries in the opening of each shell. Fold the 8-inch length of ribbon in half and knot the ends. Glue it in place on the shell for a hanging loop.

Tiny Tabletop Trees

*Whether decked with gingham bows,
yo-yos, or bright little buttons, tiny tannenbaums
make sweet holiday accents with charming
country style. Their petite size makes them
perfect for a tabletop, apartment, dorm room, or
any nook or cranny.*

Size
Trees are 8½" tall.

Materials

For Each Tree:
- ✦ Artificial evergreen tree, 7" tall
- ✦ Small amount of green reindeer moss
- ✦ Terra-cotta flowerpot, 2" tall
- ✦ Small amount of floral clay
- ✦ Buttons, bows, and jute to decorate flowerpot
- ✦ Wire cutters
- ✦ Dried or artificial flower (optional)

For Yo-yo Trees:
- ✦ Scraps of cotton fabrics in desired colors
- ✦ Assorted small buttons
- ✦ Red pearl cotton and embroidery needle
- ✦ Floral wire, 20 gauge
- ✦ Compass
- ✦ Cardboard for pattern

For Button Trees:
- ✦ Buttons in assorted sizes and shapes
- ✦ Red pearl cotton or raffia

For Bow Tree:
- ✦ Assorted scraps of holiday print fabric
- ✦ Raffia
- ✦ Pinking shears

For Scrap Tree:
- ✦ Assorted scraps of holiday print fabrics
- ✦ Pinking shears

Directions

All Trees: Remove any stand or base from the bottom of the tree, leaving only the wire stem. Cut off a few of the bottom tree branches with wire cutters, leaving about 2 inches of bare wire stem. Trim the length of the pine needles to ¼ inch on the remaining branches with scissors. Press a small amount of floral clay into the bottom of the flowerpot, then insert the tree stem into the clay. Add more clay to fill the pot. Cover the exposed clay with the dried reindeer moss. If desired, wire a dried or artificial flower to the top of the tree. Glue buttons or bows on the pot as desired or tie a jute bow to the tree stem around the base of the tree. As you work on the trees, scatter the decorations evenly around.

Yo-yo Trees: With the compass, draw a 3-inch circle on the cardboard. Cut it out and use it as a yo-yo pattern to cut about 15 circles from the fabric. Turn ¼ inch to wrong side around the edge of the circle, clip, and press (Figure 1). Using pearl cotton and the embroidery needle, hand-sew running stitches around the edge of the circle (Figure 2). Pull the thread to gather the circle and knot it to secure the gathers (Figure 3). Flatten the circle with the gathers at the center of the yo-yo (Figure 4).

We used two methods to attach the yo-yos to the trees. *Method 1:* Hold a button on top of a yo-yo and a 4-inch length of wire underneath. With pearl cotton, sew the button to the yo-yo, catching the wire below in the stitches

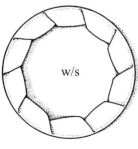

w/s

¼" edge turned under

Figure 1

r/s

Running stitches

Figure 2

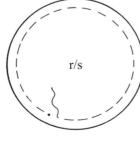

Gathered

Figure 3

Flattened

Figure 4

as you sew on the button. Twist the wire ends around a tree branch to attach the yo-yo. *Method 2:* With pearl cotton, starting from the top side and leaving a 3-inch thread end, sew through a button, then a yo-yo; holding the yo-yo in place on the branch, bring the thread under the branch, and then back up through the yo-yo and button; cut off the thread, leaving a 3-inch end. Knot the thread ends to secure the yo-yo to the tree and trim the ends to ½ inch.

Button Trees: Cut 7 inches of raffia or pearl cotton. Holding a button in place on the branch, start from the top side, thread the raffia or pearl cotton through the button, wrap under the branch, and bring up through the button to the top; tie the ends in a knot on the right side. Trim the ends to ¾ inch.

Bow Trees: With pinking shears, cut the fabric into twelve 1- by 6-inch strips. Make a bow by folding one end of the strip over the other (Figure 5). Tie the bows to the tree limbs by wrapping raffia around the branch and the bow and tying a knot at the center of the bow. Trim the raffia ends.

Scrap Trees: With pinking shears, cut the fabric into eighteen ½- by 5-inch strips. Knot the strips around the tree limbs. Trim the ends.

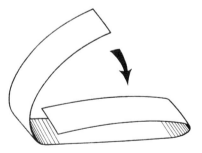

Figure 5

Queen Anne's Lace Snowflake Ornaments

With a delicacy that transcends the winter season, Queen Anne's lace is a natural choice for easy-as-a-breeze Christmas ornaments. Press as many as you like in summer for time-saving, ready-made materials during the holidays.

Size

Ornaments are about 3" in diameter.

Materials

✦ Queen Anne's lace flowers, pressed and dried (see directions)
✦ 20" length of ribbon for each ornament, ¼" wide: white or as desired
✦ Fine glitter: pearl
✦ Spray adhesive

Directions

If you are gathering your own fresh flowers over the summer, prepare them as follows: Remove the flower stems. Press the flowers in a flower press or a heavy book, letting them dry in a warm, dry place for 1 week. Store them carefully until you are ready to use them.

Spray both sides of a dried flower with adhesive and sprinkle it lightly with glitter. To make a bow hanging loop, cut a 12-inch length of ribbon and fold 4 inches at each end over the center 4 inches (see Figure 5 on this page); with a separate 8-inch length of ribbon, tie a knot around the center of the folded ribbon, leaving the streamer ends. Keeping the bow at the top, overlap the streamer ends, fold up ¼ inch, and glue the folded ends of the ribbon to the center back of the flower.

Ribbon Rose Stockings

These sleek satin-and-taffeta stockings capture the essence of Victoriana. Generous lengths of luxurious wire-edged ribbon are the easy secret to their floral charm.

Size
Stockings are 17½" tall.

Materials
For each stocking:

- ½ yd. of silk damask: cream
- 1 yd. of satin: cream
- 3¼ yd. of satin wire-edged ribbon for bow and streamers, 1½" to 2" wide: cream
- 2 yd. of satin or grosgrain wire-edged ribbon for streamers, ¾" wide: green or cream
- 2 yd. of satin or grosgrain wire-edged ribbon for rosebuds, 1½" wide: peach or dusty rose
- 1 yd. of grosgrain wire-edged ribbon for leaves and large bow (bow is optional), 1½" wide: green
- 1 yd. of chiffon ribbon for bow, 1⅜" wide: gold with solid gold edge
- 40" length of grosgrain wire-edged ribbon for large rose, 2" wide: pale peach or coral
- 20" length of grosgrain wire-edged ribbon for small rose, 1¾" wide: dusty rose or pale peach
- Matching thread and needle
- Pearl stamen clusters: white
- Dressmaker's pencil
- Toothpicks
- Clothespins
- Low-temperature glue gun and glue sticks

Directions

Note: Use the toothpicks to distribute glue in small or tight areas. Use the clothespins as extra hands while glue dries. When sewing or gluing the designs in place, attach the bottom elements, such as the leaves and bows, first.

Cutting: Enlarge the stocking pattern (see "Enlarging Patterns," page 185). Cut out a stocking front from the damask fabric. Cut 3 stocking shapes from the satin, reversing 2 of them (one reverse shape is for the stocking back and the remaining pair is for the lining).

Assembly: If desired, pin and then sew a length of 2-inch-wide cream ribbon diagonally across the upper leg on the right side of the damask front piece. With right sides of front and back together and using a ½-inch seam allowance, sew around the edges of the stocking, leaving the top edge open. Repeat for the stocking lining. Trim the seams and clip the curves. Turn the stocking right side out and press it. With wrong sides together, slip the lining inside the stocking. Turn in ½ inch around the top edges of both the lining and the stocking; topstitch the edges together. If desired, bind the top edge with 2-inch-wide cream ribbon as follows, reserving about 2⅝ yards for bows and streamers: Fold a length of the ribbon over the top edge of the stocking, turning under and overlapping the ends. Stitch in place along the edge of the ribbon.

Looped Bow: For each stocking, you will make an 8-looped bow and a 3-looped bow. Using 2 yards of 1½- to 2-inch-wide ribbon, wrap the ribbon back and forth to make 8 loops, each 4 inches long from the center

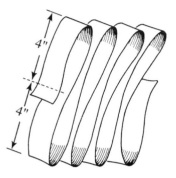

Figure 1

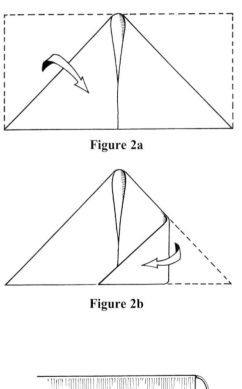

Figure 2a

Figure 2b

Ribbon

Figure 3a

(Figure 1). Wrap thread tightly around the center of the loops and knot to secure, fanning the loops out and apart to form a circle. From the same ribbon, cut one 12-inch length and one 8-inch length for streamers. Sew or glue them in place at the back of the bow. Trim the ends as desired. Using 1 yard of chiffon ribbon, wrap the ribbon in the same manner to make 3 loops, each 5 inches long from the center. Tie with thread at the center, spread the loops, and sew or glue the bow to the back of the 8-looped bow.

Folded Leaf: Make 3 to 7 leaves, as you desire. Cut 3-inch lengths of the 1½-inch-wide green ribbon for each leaf. Fold each end diagonally to the center (Figure 2a). Fold the corners at each side to the center again (Figure 2b). Gather the lower edge, if desired, and sew or glue to secure.

Gathered Roses: Make 1 large and 1 small rose. Use the 20-inch length of ribbon for the small gathered rose and the 40-inch length for the large gathered rose. Pull out about 1 inch of wire from both long edges of one end of the ribbon and twist them tightly together (Figure 3a). From the opposite end of the ribbon, gently pull the wire out of one side. Gather the ribbon tightly along this pulled wire to ruffle the ribbon (Figure 3b). Beginning at the secured end, wrap the ruffled ribbon around the stamens for the center. Continue to wrap in a loose spiral until the whole ribbon length has been used (Figure 3c). Keeping gathers in place, trim the extending pulled wire to an 8-inch end and twist this end securely around the previously twisted wire ends at the center of the rose; trim off any excess wire. Sew or glue the gathered edge to secure it.

Twisted Rosebuds: Make 2 or 3 large and 2 or 3 small rosebuds, as desired. Cut the 1½-inch satin or grosgrain ribbon into 12-inch lengths for the large rosebuds and 8-inch lengths for the small rosebuds. Fold the ribbon in half lengthwise. Hold one end between your thumb and forefinger. With your opposite hand, wrap the folded ribbon around your fingertip (Figure 4). Continue wrapping the ribbon around your finger, twisting or folding the ribbon up as shown every wrap or so to form a new petal. When the rosebud is done, with 3 or 4 wraps, slide it carefully off your finger and fold the raw edge of the ribbon to the center underside of the flower. Sew or glue the underside edges to secure them.

Finishing: Tie a large bow with the ¾-inch-wide wire-edged ribbon, making the loops large enough to be seen under the 8-looped bow and leaving long streamers. Trim the ends of the streamers as desired. Following the photograph, sew or glue the tied bow in place on the damask stocking front. Drape and attach the streamers to the stocking where desired. Attach several folded leaves, twisted rosebuds, and large gathered rose to the center front of the 8-looped bow. Sew or glue the 8-looped bow on the top of the tied bow. Arrange and attach the remaining folded leaves, small gathered rose, and rosebuds in place as desired.

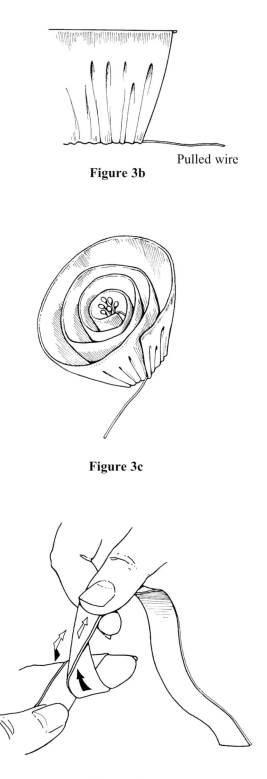

Pulled wire

Figure 3b

Figure 3c

Figure 4

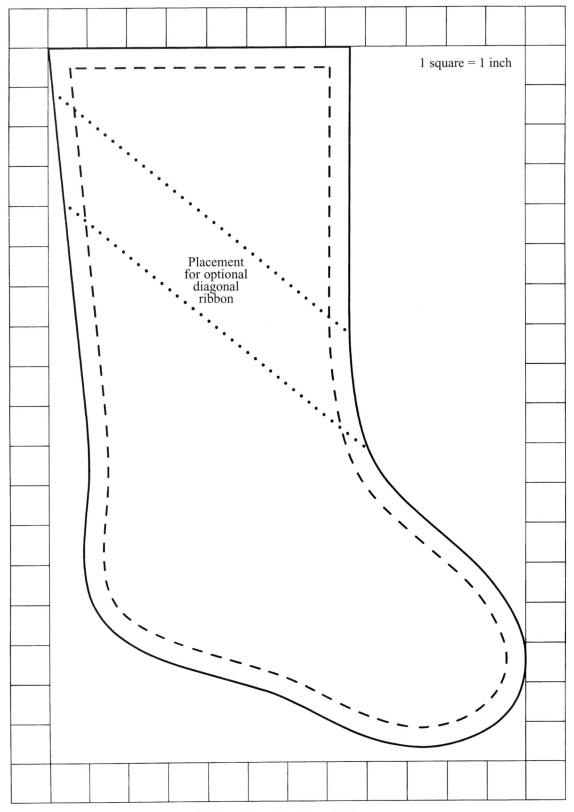

1 square = 1 inch

Placement
for optional
diagonal
ribbon

Ribbon Rose Stockings Pattern

Poinsettia Cross-stitch Table Runner

*Lavishly stitched poinsettias with
gracefully flowing bows make this table runner
an elegant holiday accent. A gift or
keepsake of heirloom quality, its handwork will
be appreciated for generations.*

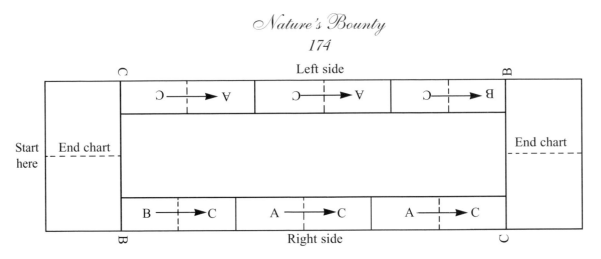

Size

Runner is 15½" × 41½".

Materials

✦ 16" × 46" piece of 27-count Linda® fabric: #264 Ivory
✦ 1 skein each of 6-strand embroidery floss (see key for colors), except 2 skeins each of Christmas Red, Coral Light
✦ 1 skein each of rayon embroidery floss, (see key for colors), except 2 skeins each of Light Topaz, Dark Topaz
✦ 1 skein each of metallic embroidery floss (see key for colors)
✦ Contrasting and matching threads
✦ ¾ oz. package of seed beads: yellow
✦ Dressmaker's pencil
✦ Embroidery hoop and needle

Directions

Cross-stitching: See "How to Cross-stitch" and "Embroidery Stitches," pages 187 and 188. With contrasting basting thread, mark the fabric's lengthwise center. Starting with end chart and one narrow end of fabric, match fabric's marked center with arrows on chart and leave 5 inches of fabric beyond the coral border line (see later for how to work the remaining edges of the runner). Following chart and key, embroider design. Work cross-stitches with 2 strands of floss over 2 vertical and 2 horizontal threads; cross-stitch coral border line with 3 strands. Work backstitches and French knots with the number of strands shown in the key. Attach seed beads with 2 strands of floss.

When end chart is done, turn fabric to work side chart along right edge as follows: Matching charts at B's, complete side chart from B to C once, then repeat from A to C twice (3 bows are worked along side edge). Then turn the fabric to work the side chart along the opposite (left) edge as follows: Starting from the embroidered end and matching the side and end charts at C, work side chart right to left from C to A twice, then work from C to B once. Now turn fabric for other end, matching B's and C's of side and end charts.

Finishing: When embroidery is done, remove the basting stitches and hand-wash the fabric in cold water. Dry it flat and press it. Mark a line 1 inch in from the edges of the table runner. To make a fringed border, pull the threads to the marked lines.

KEY

Note: *Use 1 skein of all floss colors except DMC #321 and #352 and Marlitt #839 and #1078, each of which requires 2.*

Anchor		DMC	Color
43	■	815	Garnet Medium
1006	◺	304	Christmas Red Medium
9046	✕	321	Christmas Red
11	◼	350	Coral Medium
9	╱	352	Coral Light
8	•	3824	Peach Blush
862	◢	520	Fern Green Dark
228	▼	700	Christmas Green Bright
238	⇘	703	Chartreuse
267	⋁	470	Avocado Green Light
253	∣	472	Avocado Green Ultra Light
259	•.	772	Yellow Green Very Light
278	ϲ	3819	Parrot Yellow

Center

C →

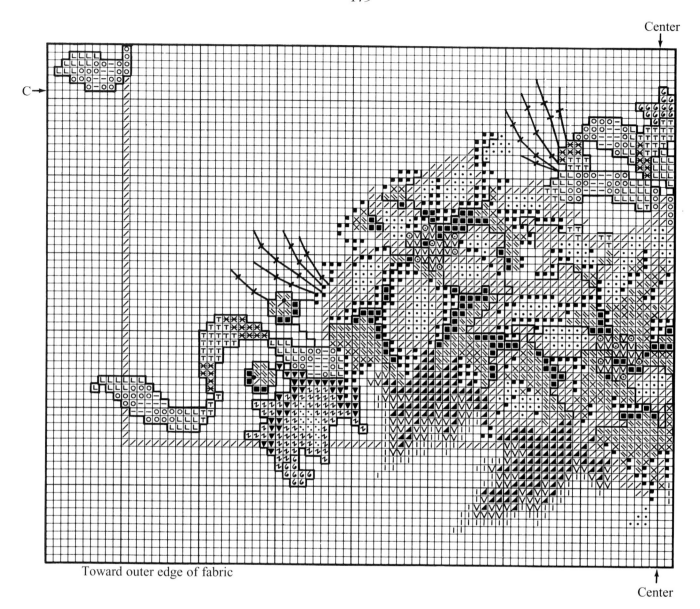

Toward outer edge of fabric

Center

Poinsettia Cross-stitch Table Runner (left section of end chart)

		Marlitt Rayon Floss	
	✕	839	Dark Topaz
	T	1079	Topaz
	L	1078	Light Topaz
	O	848	Cream
	—	1012	Off White

Anchor		DMC	Color
		BACKSTITCH (Use 1 strand)	
382	⌐	3371	Black Brown (1), ribbons
862	⌐	934	Black Avocado Green (1), poinsettia leaves
43	⌐	815	Garnet Medium (2), poinsettia veins
906	⌐	829	Golden Olive Very Dark (2), berry stems

Anchor		DMC	Color
		FRENCH KNOT (Use 2 strands, 1 wrap)	
906	●	829	Golden Olive Very Dark, berry tips
		BEADS (Use 2 strands)	
295	⊙	726	Topaz Light

		DMC #10 Metallic	
		BACKSTITCH (Use 1 strand)	
	⌐	281	Silver
		COUCHING (Use 2 strands, couched with 1 strand)	
	✛	269	Green, pine needles

Overlap from adjacent section
Center

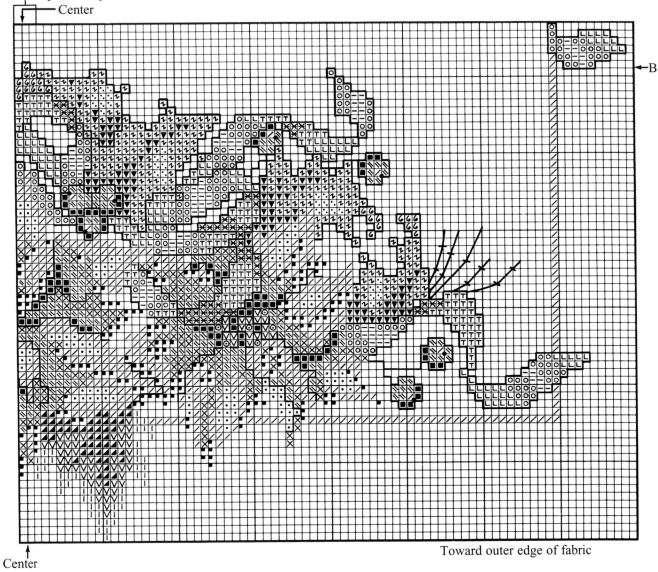

→ B

Center

Toward outer edge of fabric

Poinsettia Cross-stitch Table Runner (right section of end chart)

Anchor		DMC	Color
43	■	815	Garnet Medium
1006	◺	304	Christmas Red Medium
9046	✕	321	Christmas Red
11	▪	350	Coral Medium
9	╱	352	Coral Light
8	•	3824	Peach Blush
862	◢	520	Fern Green Dark
228	▼	700	Christmas Green Bright
238	↳	703	Chartreuse
267	V	470	Avocado Green Light
253			472	Avocado Green Ultra Light
259	•.	772	Yellow Green Very Light
278	ϭ	3819	Parrot Yellow

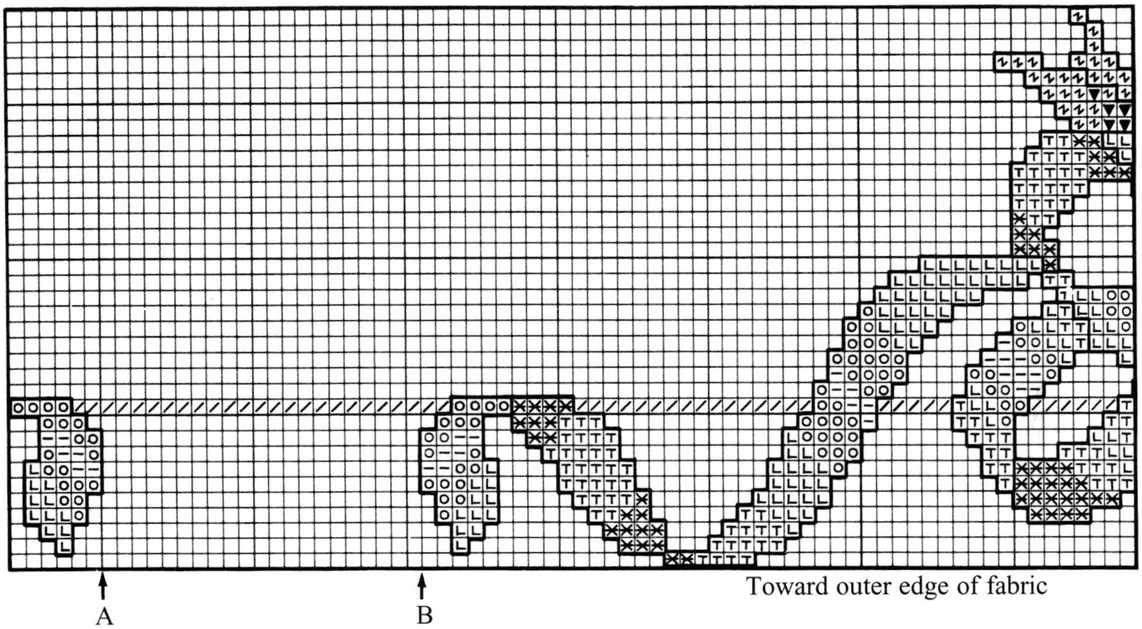

Toward outer edge of fabric

A   B

Poinsettia Cross-stitch Table Runner (left section of side chart)

	Marlitt Rayon Floss	
✗	839	Dark Topaz
T	1079	Topaz
L	1078	Light Topaz
O	848	Cream
—	1012	Off White

Anchor	DMC	Color
	BACKSTITCH (Use 1 strand)	
382	3371	Black Brown (1), ribbons
862	934	Black Avocado Green (1), poinsettia leaves
43	815	Garnet Medium (2), poinsettia veins
906	829	Golden Olive Very Dark (2), berry stems

Anchor	DMC	Color
	FRENCH KNOT (Use 2 strands, 1 wrap)	
906 ●	829	Golden Olive Very Dark, berry tips
	BEADS (Use 2 strands)	
295 ⊙	726	Topaz Light
	DMC #10 Metallic	
	BACKSTITCH (Use 1 strand)	
	281	Silver
	COUCHING (Use 2 strands, couched with 1 strand)	
✛	269	Green, pine needles

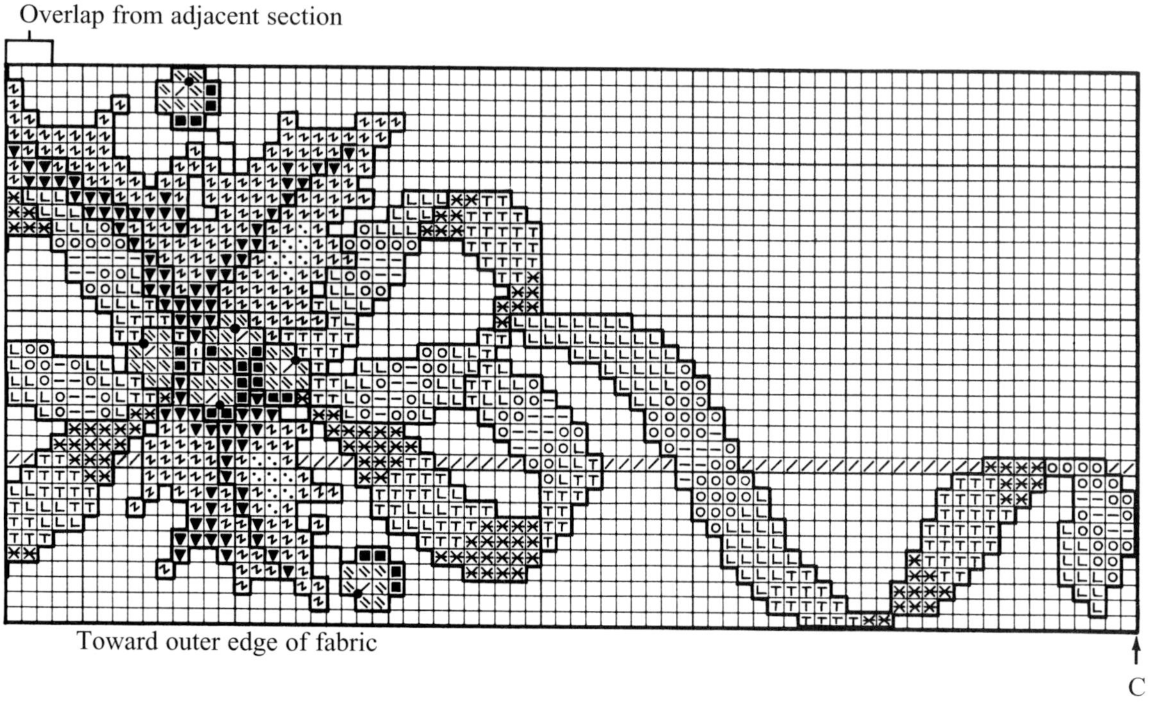

Overlap from adjacent section

Toward outer edge of fabric

C

Poinsettia Cross-stitch Table Runner (right section of side chart)

Anchor		DMC	Color
43	■	815	Garnet Medium
1006	◩	304	Christmas Red Medium
9046	✗	321	Christmas Red
11	▪	350	Coral Medium
9	╱	352	Coral Light
8	•	3824	Peach Blush
862	◢	520	Fern Green Dark
228	▼	700	Christmas Green Bright
238	⇂	703	Chartreuse
267	V	470	Avocado Green Light
253	I	472	Avocado Green Ultra Light
259	•.	772	Yellow Green Very Light
278	ι	3819	Parrot Yellow

		Marlitt Rayon Floss	
	✗	839	Dark Topaz
	T	1079	Topaz
	L	1078	Light Topaz
	O	848	Cream
	—	1012	Off White

Anchor		DMC	Color
		BACKSTITCH (Use 1 strand)	
382	⌐	3371	Black Brown (1), ribbons
862	⌐	934	Black Avocado Green (1), poinsettia leaves
43	⌐	815	Garnet Medium (2), poinsettia veins
906	⌐	829	Golden Olive Very Dark (2), berry stems
		FRENCH KNOT (Use 2 strands, 1 wrap)	
906	●	829	Golden Olive Very Dark, berry tips
		BEADS (Use 2 strands)	
295		726	Topaz Light

		DMC #10 Metallic	
		BACKSTITCH (Use 1 strand)	
281			Silver
		COUCHING (Use 2 strands, couched with 1 strand)	
269			Green, pine needles

Poinsettia Ribbon
Napkin Rings

*Dress up any holiday dinner setting with vivid
napkin rings cleverly crafted from
wire-edged ribbon. Quickly fashioned and easily
finished, they make wonderful last-minute
decorations or party favors.*

Size
Ring is 2" in diameter.

Materials
- 1½ yd. of wire-edged ombré ribbon for each ring, 1½" wide: red
- 1 yd. wire-edged ombré ribbon for each ring, ⅞" wide: red
- Matching heavy-duty thread and needle
- Artificial holly leaves
- Beads, about 9 mm: gold metallic
- Toothpicks
- Clothespins
- Cardboard roll from paper towels
- Low-temperature glue gun and glue sticks

Directions
Note: Use the toothpicks to distribute glue in small or tight areas. Use the clothespins as extra hands while glue dries.

Poinsettia: Cut the wide ribbon into 8-inch lengths. Fold the ribbon in half crosswise. With darker section of the ombré ribbon at the top, fold each end diagonally to the front (Figure 1); finger-press. Unfold the ends. Using the creases as a guide, sew a running stitch along the creases at the short ends and across the connecting edge of the ribbon (Figure 2). Trim excess ribbon at the corners, leaving a ⅛-inch seam allowance. Pull the thread to gather the ribbon slightly (Figure 3), then knot the thread to secure the gathers. Open the unsewn edges and pinch the ribbon into a petal shape (Figure 4). Make 6 petals for each ring. Arrange the petals to form a flower; sew the points together at the center.

Assembly: Cut the cardboard roll into 1-inch widths for the rings. Glue one end of the narrow ribbon to the ring and bring the ribbon through the center of the ring. Continue to wrap the ribbon around the ring, covering it completely and overlapping the edges on each round. Turn under the end on the last wrap and glue it to the inside of the ring. Glue 2 artificial holly leaves in place under the poinsettia petals, then glue the poinsettia to the ring. Glue a cluster of gold beads in the center of the flower.

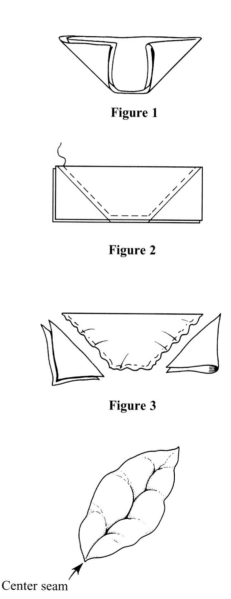

Figure 1

Figure 2

Figure 3

Center seam

Figure 4

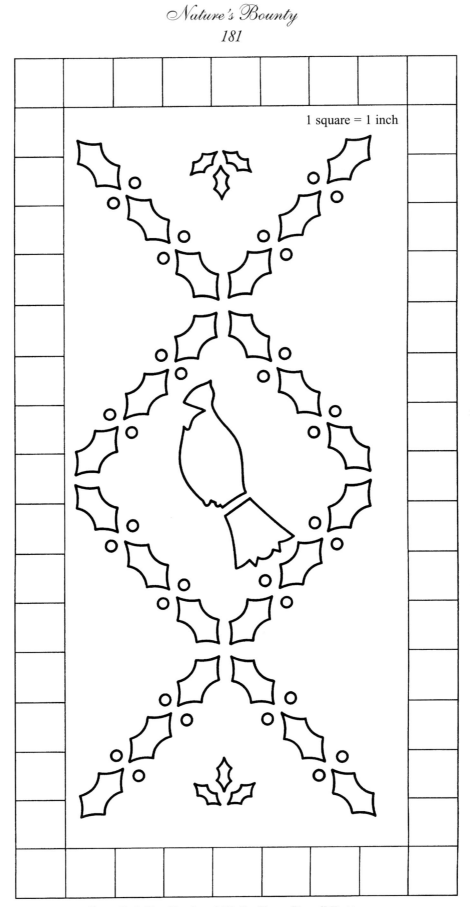

1 square = 1 inch

Stenciled Cardinal and Holly Tray Stencil Pattern

Stenciled Cardinal and Holly Tray

Striking red cardinals complement holly leaves and berries on this handsome tray—perfect for serving holiday treats. One of the most popular plants of the season, holly often adorns everything from the entryway to the Christmas pudding.

Size
Tray is 16" × 21".

Materials
+ 16" × 21" wooden tray
+ Acrylic paint: antique gold, pure gold, holiday red, tartan green, cream, and black
+ Foam paintbrush, 2" wide
+ Stencil brushes, ½" diameter
+ Stencil paper
+ Fine and medium sandpaper and tack cloth
+ Natural sponge
+ Tracing and transfer papers
+ Paper punch
+ Crafts knife
+ Rubber cement
+ Spray sealer

Directions
Note: Cover the work surface with newspaper and plastic wrap and keep a roll of paper towels handy. Allow the paints to dry thoroughly between steps.

View of the back for
CASSINA and SERPENT
Chiswick Gardens

Painting: Sand the tray with the medium sandpaper, then the fine; wipe with the tack cloth. Using the foam brush, paint the sides of the tray with 2 coats of antique gold. Paint the bottom tray surface with 2 coats of cream. Dip the sponge in pure gold, blotting any excess paint onto a paper towel, and lightly dab the entire tray to create a stippled effect.

Stenciling: Enlarge and transfer the cardinal and holly design onto the stencil paper (see "Enlarging Patterns" and "Making Stencils," pages 185 and 186). Make a separate stencil for the bird details; they are given actual size and can be traced directly onto stencil paper. See Figure 1 for the placement of the bird details. Cut out the stencils. Use the paper punch to cut out the berries. Cover the back of the stencil paper with rubber cement. Allow to dry.

Before you begin your project, practice on scrap paper, working as follows: Blot any excess paint from the brush onto a paper towel. Stamp the brush in an up-and-down motion to achieve a crisp, clean edge. Working from the edges of the stencil opening toward the center, leave the center blank, lightly colored, or solidly colored, as desired. To prevent smears, allow paints to dry and be sure the stencil edges are not wet when you move the stencil. When you are comfortable with your results, you are ready to begin your project.

Following the photograph, stencil the design 3 times across the width of the tray surface. Stencil a cardinal in each complete diamond and turn the stencil to add small holly leaves in the triangles along the side edges of the tray surface. Paint the cardinal and the berries holiday red, the holly tartan green, the bird face black, and the bird beak, the feet, and the branch antique gold. Paint a dot of antique gold for the bird's eye. Spray-paint the entire tray with 2 coats of sealer.

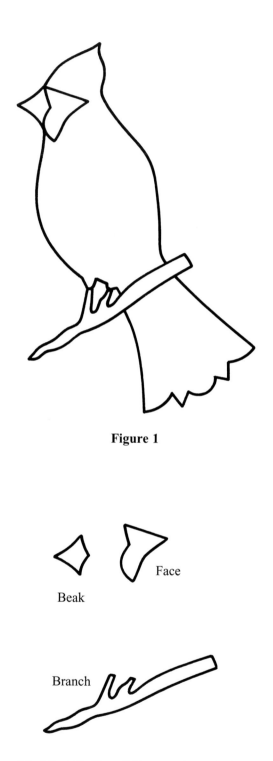

Figure 1

Beak

Face

Branch

Bird Details Stencil Pattern (actual size)

Basic Techniques

The Workroom

We would all love to have a Santa's workshop we could escape to right in our homes. Who hasn't lamented, "If I only had a better place to work (and more time), I'd make all my Christmas presents and decorations"? While we may not have the space and finances to accommodate that wish, a well-equipped work space does make crafting more enjoyable and more efficient.

Even if your work space is a small spot in the basement, part of the dining room table, or a corner of your bedroom, if you are organized and prepared, your work will go smoothly. Here are some tips:

✶ It is important that your work area be well lit and that you have a clean, clear surface to work on. For messy projects and projects involving paint, we recommend covering the work surface with newspaper and then covering the paper with plastic wrap.

✶ Be sure to work in a well-ventilated area, especially when doing projects that involve paint or spray coatings. Carefully dispose of paint rags or papers to prevent a fire hazard.

✶ For sewing projects, we assume you have a sewing machine, but if you don't, some of the smaller projects (such as the Velvet Santa Star Ornaments, pages 30–32) could be sewn by hand. You will also need an iron and an ironing board.

✶ Always have on hand the following items: typewriter paper, tracing paper, sharp pencils, scissors, masking tape, cellophane tape, white glue or glue sticks, a crafts knife and extra blades, a stylus or nonworking ballpoint pen, pinking shears, tape measure, straightedge, and rubber gloves.

✶ When cutting with a crafts knife, use a self-healing cutting mat as a work surface.

The Basics

Fabrics

The amount of fabric specified for the projects is for 44- to 45-inch-wide fabric, unless otherwise noted. If you use fabric that is narrower or wider, you will need to adjust the amount of fabric you purchase accordingly.

Enlarging Patterns

If you do not wish to write directly in your book, make a photocopy of the patterns you want to enlarge, being careful to hold the book flat against the machine to prevent any distortion. Using a ruler and a pencil, extend the grid lines over the pattern. On paper, draw a grid of squares that are the size given by the scale with the diagram (for example, if 1 square is equal to 1", you should draw a grid with 1-inch squares). Be sure your grid has the same number of rows and columns of squares as the original. (Paper already printed with 1-inch grids can also be purchased at many art and stationery stores.) For small projects you can use graph paper, following the 1-inch markings to enlarge. Refer to the pattern and mark the full-size grid where the pattern lines intersect the grid lines. Connect the markings, then refine any details if necessary.

Photocopy Enlargment: You can also use a photocopying machine to enlarge a pattern, but it may take some trial and error to determine the correct percentage. Be sure to measure your grid to verify that it is the size that is called for.

Transferring Patterns

To transfer actual-size patterns from the book, or enlarged patterns that you want to preserve, make a photocopy of the pattern or use tracing paper and pencil to trace it. On the patterns, the outer solid line is the cutting line, and, when indicated, the inner broken line is the seamline.

Half-pattern: If the pattern you wish to transfer is given as a half-pattern, fold the fabric and place the marked center line on the fold to cut through both layers. You also can make a full pattern by folding tracing paper in half and tracing the design onto each side with the center line on the fold.

Pattern Outline Only: If you need only the outline of the actual-size or enlarged shape, cut out the pattern, position and pin or tape it to your material, and cut it out; if the shape is intricate, you should draw around it with a soft pencil or a dressmaker's pencil (for fabrics) before cutting to ensure an accurate outline.

Templates: If you are using the same pattern several times, make a sturdy template from cardboard or flat plastic. Trace and cut out the pattern; draw around the shape on cardboard or plastic with a marker. Cut out with strong scissors or a crafts knife.

Pattern Details: If your pattern has details, transfer the design before cutting, using transfer paper (available at art supply stores), dress-maker's carbon (nonstaining on fabrics), or carbon paper (on paper or wood). Position the pattern face up where desired on your material. Slip the transfer paper between the paper pattern and the material with the carbon side against the material. Trace the pattern lines with a stylus or a nonworking ballpoint pen to transfer the design. Freehand marks for names or fine details can be added to fabrics with tailor's chalk or a dressmaker's pencil.

Transferring to Wrong Side or Fusible Web: When designs are to be transferred to the wrong side of the fabric or to fusible web, you must reverse the design (except for Victorian Crazy-Quilt Stocking, page 25, which has already reversed patterns). Use a fine marker to trace the design as printed onto tracing paper, then turn the tracing paper over. If you cannot see the drawing well from the reverse side, hold the tracing against a sunny window and retrace the design on the reverse side of the paper. With the reverse side up, place the tracing over transfer paper and draw over the lines to transfer the design as before.

There are also special dressmaker's or embroiderer's pens that allow you to trace a design and iron the tracing, drawn side down, on the wrong side of the fabric. This easily reverses the design on the back of the fabric so that the right side will be properly oriented.

Making Stencils

Enlarge the stencil design if necessary, using a pen or fine-line marker with permanent ink to mark the design lines. Using a pencil, trace the design onto stencil paper, which is available at craft supply stores. Work over a light box or hold papers against a sunny window to help in tracing the design. (If you intend to use a stencil many times, you should use a more durable stencil material such as Mylar or acetate, using a marker for transferring the cutting design onto the plastic. Be sure to wipe the stencil clean after cutting it.) Transfer all register marks to the stencils.

Cut out the stencil with a crafts knife with a sharp blade. Blades come either pointed or curved, and you should try both to see which you prefer. Protect your work surface with a self-healing mat or with a board. Work with the stencil paper right side up. Cut the small shapes first. Pull the knife toward you when cutting, rather than pushing it away. Bear down with enough even pressure to cut the paper, but don't tire your hand by applying unnecessary force. Curves are cut most easily by turning the stencil (or the whole mat, if you're using a small one) rather than the knife. Be careful at corners not to extend the cuts beyond the design line. Mistakes can be patched with tape and recut.

Dyeing with Tea

Tea staining is an easy and authentic way to give new-looking fabrics an antique appearance. Before chemical dyes were widely available, loose tea was one of the natural dye stuffs our ancestors used to color fabrics and yarns. Today we have tea bags to make the process as easy as brewing a cup of tea.

Several of the projects in this book call for tea-stained muslin. For items requiring small pieces of fabric, simply boil a cup of water and steep 3 tea bags for 5 minutes. Remove the tea bags from the water and discard them. Soak the muslin in the tea for 20 minutes. Wring out the fabric, rinse it in cold water, and press it. For larger pieces of fabric, increase the amount of water and the number of tea bags proportionately.

How to Cross-stitch

Use an evenweave fabric. To prevent raveling, whipstitch the raw edges. If you wish, place the fabric in an embroidery hoop to keep it taut while stitching, but to avoid creases, do not leave it in the hoop when you're not working on it. Cut the floss into 18-inch lengths; separate the strands into the number of strands specified. Use a tapestry needle. Do not knot your thread.

On Aida cloth, each cross-stitch is made over the intersection of 1 vertical and 1 horizontal thread on the fabric (see Figure 1). Always pass the needle through the "holes," not the threads. Begin by bringing the needle up through the fabric, leaving a 1-inch strand of floss on the back. Hold this strand in the direction you are stitching; secure it by stitching over it. On other evenweave fabrics, work the stitches over 2 threads vertically and 2 threads horizontally (see Figure 2).

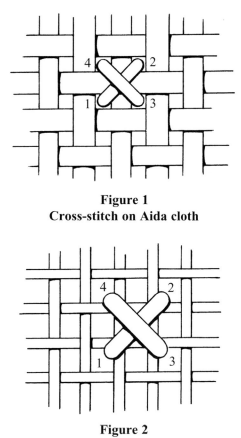

Figure 1
Cross-stitch on Aida cloth

Figure 2
Cross-stitch on other evenweave fabric

The cross-stitch is made in two steps: You form an × by passing the floss diagonally across the fabric threads in two directions (Figures 1 and 2). Be sure that all underlying stitches slant diagonally in one direction and that all top stitches slant in the opposite direction. When making a row of adjacent stitches in the same color, first work all the underlying stitches of the × as many times as required, then work back, crossing all the stitches with the top stitches. When making adjacent stitches, pass the needle through the same hole more than once. To secure the end of the floss, slide the needle under several stitches on the back of the work and snip the excess floss. Do not carry floss across the back from one color area to another.

Each square on a cross-stitch chart represents 1 cross-stitch; refer to the color key to match the thread numbers to the different symbols on the chart. Do not repeat stitches in marked overlap rows. Backstitches (see "Embroidery Stitches," below) are indicated by straight lines on the chart. See the following stitch diagrams for other stitches indicated on the charts and in project directions.

Embroidery Stitches

A number of projects use specific embroidery stitches, such as French knots and lazy-daisy stitches. Follow the how-to diagrams for the correct needle and thread placement to work the desired stitches. The Victorian Crazy-Quilt Stocking (page 25) calls for a number of embroidered edges. Use the stitches and the border patterns shown, or use your own favorite stitches, combining several different stitches and colors in each border.

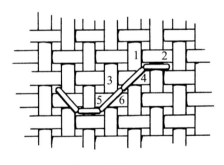

Backstitch

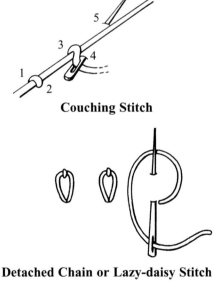

Couching Stitch

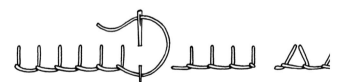

Blanket and Slanted Buttonhole Stitches

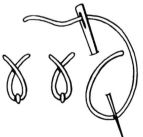

Detached Chain or Lazy-daisy Stitch

Variation of Slanted Buttonhole Stitch

Detached Twisted Chain Stitch

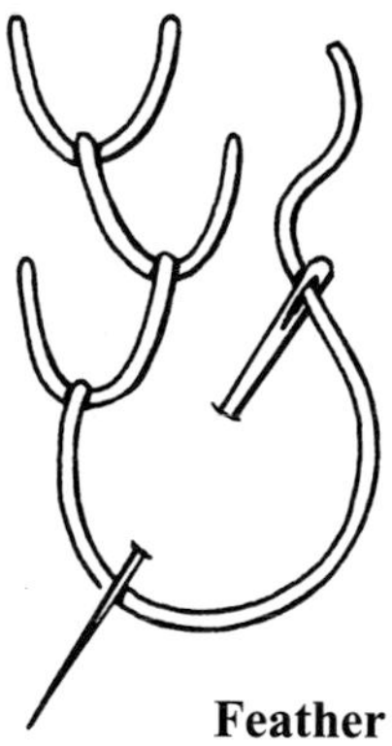

Feather Stitch

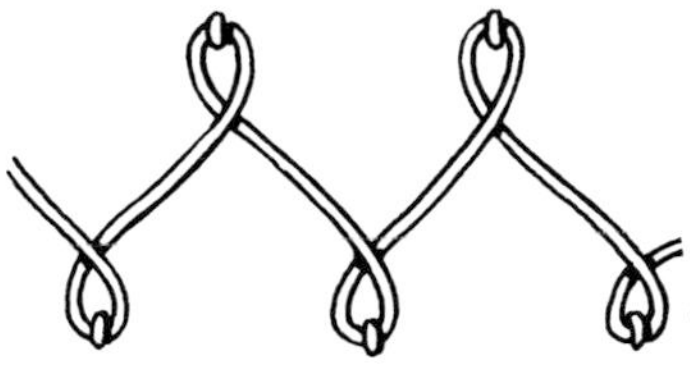

Looped and Couched Stitch

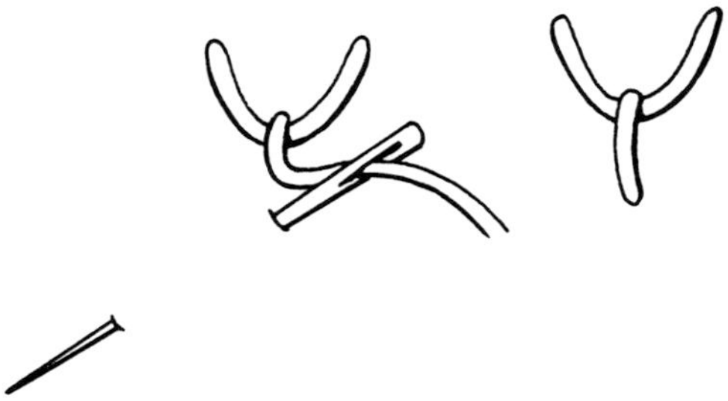

Fly Stitch

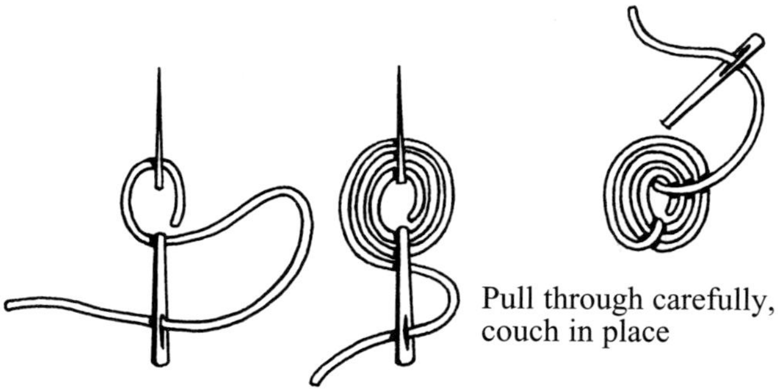

Rosette Stitch

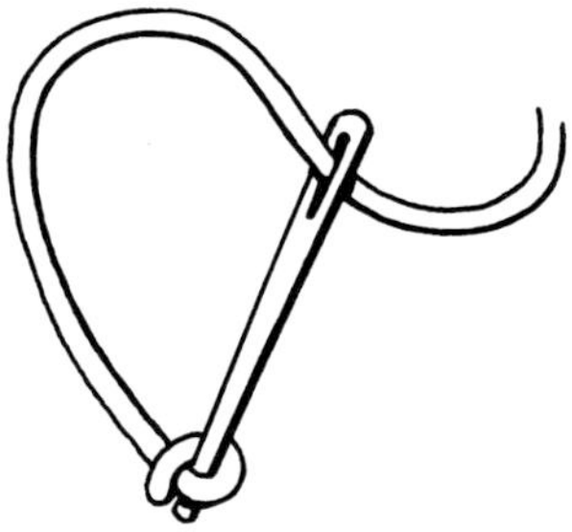

Pull through carefully,
couch in place

French Knot

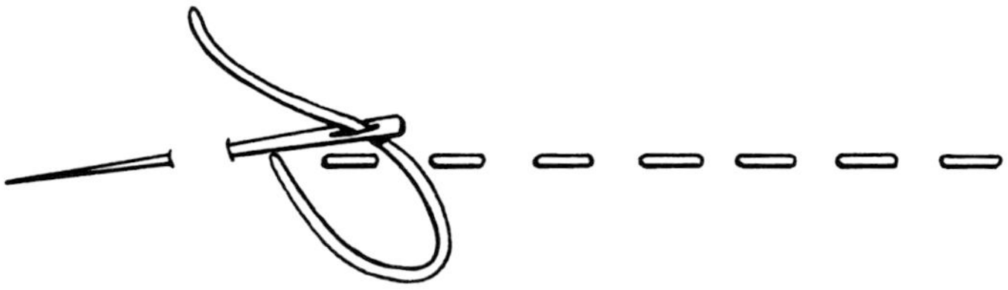

Running Stitch

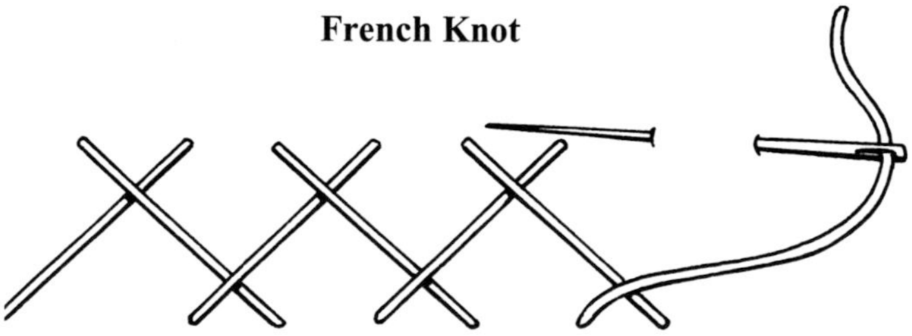

Herringbone Stitch

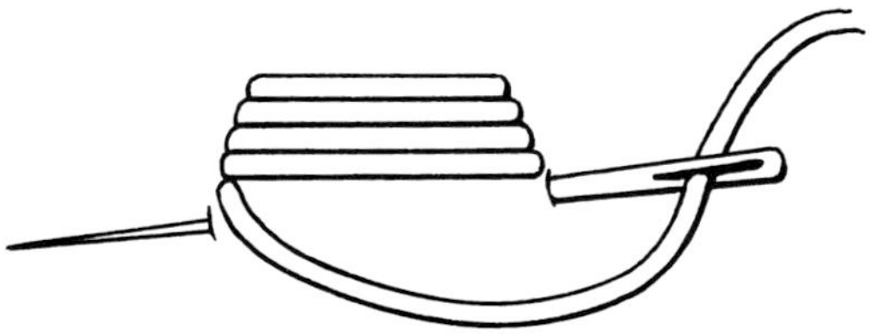

Satin Stitch

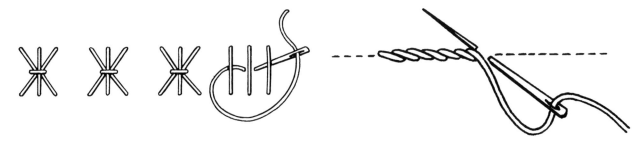

Sheaf Stitch   **Stem Stitch**

Star Stitch

Variations and Combinations

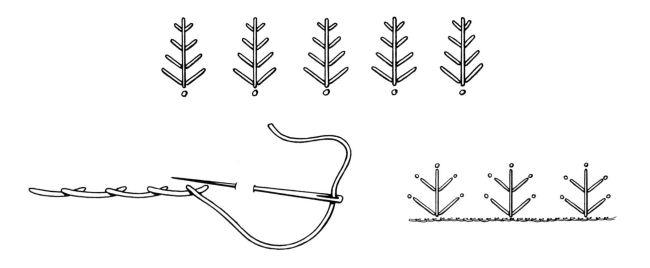

Sources

Most of the materials called for in the directions for the projects in this
book are available in craft stores. If you have difficulty finding specific items,
contact the manufacturer for a listing of suppliers in your area.

Accent Products
(Craft paints)
100 North Street
Bloomsbury, NJ 08804
(800) 877-3165

Anchor/Marlitt Floss
Coats & Clark, Inc.
Consumer Service Dept.
P.O. Box 27067
Greenville, SC 29616
(800) 648-1479

Birdhouse Enterprises
(Punch-needle supplies)
Send self-addressed, stamped
business envelope to:
110 Jennings Avenue
Dept. OFCC
Patchogue, NY 11772

Charles Craft
(Cross-stitch fabrics)
P.O. Box 1049
Laurinburg, NC 28353
(800) 346-4721

DMC Corporation
(Embroidery floss)
To order, contact:
Herrschners Inc.
2800 Hoover Road
Stevens Point, WI 54481
(800) 441-0838

The Gifted Line
(Angel stickers and gift wrap)
For stores nearest you call:
(510) 215-4777 *or*
(800) 5-GIFTED

Hartstone
(Angel molds)
1719 Dearborn Street
P.O. Box 2626
Zanesville, OH 43702
(614) 452-9000

Kate's Paperie
(Special papers)
561 Broadway
New York, NY 10012
(212) 941-9816

Kreinik Mfg.
(Embroidery threads)
P.O. Box 1966
Parkersburg, WV 26102
(800) 624-1928

Mills Floral
(Dried flowers and pods)
4550 Peachtree Lakes Drive
Duluth, GA 30136
(404) 729-8995

Offray Ribbons
Route 24, P.O. Box 601
Chester, NJ 07930
(908) 879-4700

Plaid Enterprises
(Craft paints)
P.O. Box 7600
Norcross, GA 30091-7600
(404) 923-8200

The Pottery Barn
(Wooden trays)
Mail Order Department
P.O. Box 7044
San Francisco, CA 94120-7044
(800) 922-5507

Prym Dritz
(Fray Check™)
P.O. Box 5028
Spartanburg, SC 29304

Tulip
(Craft paints)
24 Prime Park Way
Natick, MA 01760
(800) 458-7010

Wichelt Imports
(Embroidery threads and fabrics)
To order, call:
The Universal Stitcher
(800) 830-5027

Zweigart
(Even-weave fabrics)
Contact: Rosemary Drysdale
80 Long Lane
East Hampton, NY 11937
(516) 324-1705

ACKNOWLEDGMENTS We would like to thank the following designers for their wonderful imagination and extraordinary efforts in creating the projects in this book: **Yvonne Beecher:** *Happy Holidays Sampler;* **Beverly Karcher:** *Hooked Santa Picture, Victorian Crazy-Quilt Stocking;* **Nancy Keller for C. M. Offray:** *Poinsettia Ribbon Napkin Rings;* **Karin Lidbeck:** *Heavenly Screen Angels, Littlest Angel Photo Ornament, Stencil Star Stocking, Victorian Print Ornaments, Santa Claus Stocking;* **Ursula Michael:** *Glory to God Pillow, Angelic Wrappings;* **Sunny O'Neil:** *Fleece Father Christmas, Pinecone Topiary, Rag Topiary, Queen Anne's Lace Snowflake Ornaments;* **Susan Piatt:** *Dutch Colonial Gingerbread House;* **Barbara Sestok:** *Nativity Sampler, Poinsettia Cross-stitch Table Runner;* **Ginger Hansen Shafer:** *Golden Angels Table Runner, Flying Brass Angels, Molded-Paper Angels, Twinkling Star Tree Skirt, Five Shining Celestial Ornaments, Wire Mesh Vase and Votive Holders, Nativity Paper Cuts (Stained Glass), Three Wise Men, Painted Tray, Pinecone Father Christmas, Father Christmas Cornucopias, Theorem-Painted Santa Stocking, Christmas Toy Box, Foil Star Ornaments, Topiary Bear, Popcorn Cones, Wooden Blocks, Decoupage Fruit Plates, Fruitful Gift Wraps, Fruit and Ribbon Ornaments, Dough Ornaments, Strawberry Jewel Ornament, Stenciled Cardinal and Holly Tray, Zinnia Topiary, Musical Trees, Dowel Pyramid Tree, Golden Shell Ornaments, Flower-Stamped Wraps, Ribbons, and Cards, Floral Cut-Paper Wreath;* **Mimi Shimmin:** *Skating Party Banner, Nutcracker Stocking;* **Jaqueline Smyth:** *Velvet Santa Star Ornaments, Topsy-Turvy Doll, Tiny Tabletop Trees;* **Mirinda Stewart for C. M. Offray:** *Ribbon Rose Stockings.*

Index